P9-EDF-964

THE GOSPELS
OF THE MARGINALIZED

The Gospels
of the Marginalized

THE REDEMPTION OF DOUBTING THOMAS, MARY MAGDALENE, AND JUDAS ISCARIOT IN EARLY CHRISTIAN LITERATURE

Marvin W. Meyer

CASCADE *Books* · Eugene, Oregon

270
MEY

THE GOSPELS OF THE MARGINALIZED
The Redemption of Doubting Thomas, Mary Magdalene, and Judas
Iscariot in Early Christian Literature

Copyright © 2012 Marvin W. Meyer. All rights reserved. Except for brief
quotations in critical publications or reviews, no part of this book may
be reproduced in any manner without prior written permission from the
publisher. Write: Permissions, Wipf and Stock Publishers, 199 W. 8th Ave.,
Suite 3, Eugene, OR 97401.

Cascade Books
An Imprint of Wipf and Stock Publishers
199 W. 8th Ave., Suite 3
Eugene, OR 97401
www.wipfandstock.com

ISBN 13: 978-1-62032-268-0

Cataloging-in-Publication data:

Meyer, Marvin W.
    The gospels of the marginalized : the redemption of doubting Thomas, Mary
Magdalene, and Judas Iscariot in early Christian literature / Marvin W. Meyer.

    x + 156 p.; 21.5 cm.—Includes bibliographic references and index.

    ISBN 13: 978-1-62032-268-0

    1. Gospel of Thomas (Coptic Gospel)—Criticism, interpretation, etc. 2. Gospel
of Mary—Criticism, interpretation, etc. 3. Gospel of Judas—Criticism, interpretation,
etc. 4. Gnosticism. 5.Gnosticism—Sources. 6. Christian literature, Early—History and
criticism. I. Title.

BT1390 M49 2012

Manufactured in the USA

HELENA COLLEGE
University of Montana
LIBRARY
1115 N.Roberts
Helena, MT 59601

"Whoever discovers what these sayings mean
will not taste death."

—Gospel of Thomas saying 1

CONTENTS

PREFACE

Uncovering the truth behind the fiction of Thomas the doubting disciple, Mary Magdalene the repentant prostitute, and Judas Iscariot the vile betrayer of Jesus in the gospel stories is the task I undertake. Through scholarly research and discussions with colleagues and students, it has become apparent to me that these three prominent characters in the Jesus drama have been interpreted in ways they do not deserve, in the interests of telling a memorable story or making a theological point or finding someone to blame for the horrible death of Jesus. The discovery and publication of three astonishing gospels, the Gospel of Thomas, the Gospel of Mary, and the Gospel of Judas, with strikingly different depictions of Thomas, Mary, and Judas, provides a fitting occasion for reexamining the careers of these three followers of Jesus, as their lives are portrayed in the New Testament gospels, the Gospels of Thomas, Mary, and Judas, and other early Christian texts. Such an undertaking promises to yield exciting and refreshing insights into the story of Jesus.

I would like to offer my thanks to K. C. Hanson, Heather Carraher, and their colleagues at Cascade Books for encouragement and help in publishing this book. They have been consistently congenial and professional as we have worked together. The Griset Chair in Bible and Christian Studies at Chapman University continues to offer generous support for my research. I acknowledge the colleagues, students, and friends who have engaged me over the course of a generation as I—and we—have tried to come to terms with these texts and traditions from the literature of early Christianity. My wife and children endured, with grace and humor, a frequently preoccupied bearded presence floating through the days of their lives, and for that I am grateful. And I offer a virtual libation of thankfulness to be poured, as it were, into the sands of Egypt, sands which have faithfully preserved so many texts lost for centuries but discovered in our day, for our enjoyment and enlightenment.

1

INTRODUCTION

Doubting Thomas, Mary Magdalene, Judas Iscariot: The very names of these disciples conjure up images in Christian tradition of bad faith, questionable morality, and wicked betrayal.[1] In the New Testament gospels, to be sure, all the disciples have moments of doubt and uncertainty, and Peter himself denies vehemently and profanely that he knows Jesus on the eve of the crucifixion. Yet within the New Testament and early church history, Thomas, Mary, and Judas are shunned and ostracized in particular ways and for particular reasons. In the Gospel of John, Thomas is doubting Thomas, the stubborn disciple who will not believe until he touches the wounds of the crucified and raised Jesus. According to the Gospel of Luke chapter 8, Mary Magdalene has to be cleansed by Jesus of demon possession (she is a woman, it is suggested, with psychological or social problems), and in the late sixth century Pope Gregory the Great equated her (wrongly) with the unnamed prostitute of Luke 7, so that thereafter Mary Magdalene is thought to be a repentant prostitute—repentant, but a prostitute nonetheless. It is no wonder that she cannot break into the circle of the Twelve in most of Christian tradition. And Judas Iscariot remains one of the most vilified of all the characters in human history.

1. This introduction is based on a series of presentations I have given, at several locales around the world, in the wake of the announcement and publication of the Gospel of Judas and Codex Tchacos in 2006 and 2007. My thanks to the National Geographic Society for their support and to host institutions for their collegiality.

Didn't he turn his friend, perhaps his best friend, over to the Roman authorities to be crucified? Didn't he do so with a kiss—the Judas kiss? Is there anything more heinous and reprehensible than that?

Hence, Thomas, Mary Magdalene, and Judas Iscariot have commonly been marginalized as followers of Jesus—at least until recent times. In the past century or so, several early Christian gospels have been discovered in the sands of Egypt, and these newly recovered texts have begun to shed important new light on the early church and the roles of disciples of Jesus in early Christian communities. According to these gospels, Thomas, Mary Magdalene, and Judas Iscariot may be viewed in a more positive way than traditionally has been the case. Thomas may be understood as the guarantor of the sayings of Jesus, Mary may be a beloved disciple, and Judas may be reconsidered as the one who knew Jesus best and who is the recipient of revelations about God and the world from the master.

The Gospels of Thomas, Mary, and Judas have all come to the attention of scholars and other interested readers in the past few years, and since their discovery they have suggested exciting new possibilities for how we may choose to read and interpret the history of the Christian movement—from the earliest days until the present.

❧

Around the end of 1945, the texts known as the Nag Hammadi library were discovered, not at the city of Nag Hammadi itself, but near the base of a majestic cliff, the Jabal al-Tarif, which flanks the Nile River a few kilometers from Nag Hammadi.[2] Among the texts in the Nag Hammadi library was a Coptic translation of the Gospel of Thomas, an early Christian gospel known from a few

2. On the stories of the discovery of the Nag Hammadi library, cf. Doresse, *The Secret Books of the Egyptian Gnostics*; Meyer, *The Gnostic Discoveries*, 15–19; Meyer, *The Nag Hammadi Scriptures*, 1–5; Robinson, "From the Cliff to Cairo"; Robinson, "Nag Hammadi: The First Fifty Years."

citations in the church fathers and, as it turns out, Greek papyrus fragments uncovered in an ancient rubbish heap at Oxyrhynchus in Egypt. The villages closest to the Jabal al-Tarif bear the names Hamra Dum, al-Busa, al-Dabba (the site of the Monastery of the Angel, Deir al-Malak), al-Qasr (the site of the Pachomian monastery at Chenoboskion), and Faw Qibli (the site of the Pachomian monastery at Pbow). Five years after the discovery, the French scholar Jean Doresse explored the region and tried to find out the circumstances of the discovery of the Nag Hammadi library. He published his story in his book, *The Secret Books of the Egyptian Gnostics*. According to Doresse, he spoke with some people from the area, and they directed him to the southern part of an ancient cemetery. They reported that peasants from Hamra Dum and al-Dabba, searching for manure to fertilize their fields, found somewhere near this locale a large jar filled with papyri bound in the form of books. Doresse writes,

> The vase was broken and nothing remains of it; the manuscripts were taken to Cairo and no one knows what then became of them. As to the exact location of the find, opinion differed by some few dozen yards; but everyone was sure that it was just about here. And from the ground itself we shall learn nothing more; it yields nothing but broken bones, fragments of cloth without interest, and some potsherds.[3]

He concludes,

> We have never been able to discover exactly where the Coptic Manichaean manuscripts came from, nor the *Pistis-Sophia*, nor the Bruce Codex. So it was well worth the trouble to find out, in a pagan cemetery a few miles from Chenoboskion, the exact site of one of the most voluminous finds of ancient literature; thus to be a little better able to place this library in the frame of history to which it belongs; and to support, with concordant details, the hypotheses that have been made about its antiquity.[4]

3. Doresse, *The Secret Books of the Egyptian Gnostics*, 133.
4. Ibid., 136.

James M. Robinson has offered another version of the story of the discovery.[5] For a number of years, Robinson conducted interviews with people from the towns and villages in the Nag Hammadi area, in particular Muhammad Ali of the al-Samman clan, a resident of al-Qasr, and from the interviews he pieced together a fascinating account of how the Nag Hammadi codices were uncovered—an account many of us find more convincing than that of Doresse. Where possible, Robinson attempted to confirm dates and events from official records. As Robinson has reconstructed the story, the discovery of the Nag Hammadi library took place in about December of 1945, when several Egyptian fellahin—including Muhammad Ali, his brothers Khalifah Ali and Abu al-Magd, and others—were riding their camels to the Jabal al-Tarif in order to gather *sabakh*, the natural fertilizer from manure that typically accumulates around there. They hobbled their camels at the foot of the Jabal, the account continues, and began to dig around a large boulder on the talus, or slope of debris, that has formed against the cliff face. As they were digging, they unexpectedly came upon a large storage jar buried by the boulder, with a bowl sealed on the mouth of the jar as a lid. Apparently the youngest of the brothers, Abu al-Magd, initially uncovered the jar, but Muhammad Ali, as the oldest of the brothers, took control of the operation. In his account of what transpired, Muhammad Ali has suggested to Robinson that he paused before removing the lid or breaking open the jar, out of fear that the jar might contain a jinni, or spirit, that could cause trouble if released from the jar. It seems that Muhammad Ali also recalled stories of hidden treasures buried in Egypt, and his love of gold overcame his fear of jinn. He smashed the jar with his mattock, and indeed something golden in color and glistening in the sunlight—fragments of papyrus, we might conclude—flew out of the jar and disappeared into the air. And when he looked into the broken jar to see what remained, he found only a collection of old books—the codices of the Nag Hammadi library.

---

5. Cf. Robinson, "From the Cliff to Cairo"; Robinson, "Nag Hammadi: The First Fifty Years."

Robinson's version of the story is carefully documented, and it includes colorful anecdotes and detailed accounts of events. For instance, Robinson reminisces about how he persuaded Muhammad Ali to return to the site of the discovery, so close to Hamra Dum, where a family caught up in acts of vengeance with the family of Muhammad Ali lived. Robinson recalls,

> I had to go to Hamra Dum myself, find the son of Ahmad Isma'il, the man Muhammad Ali had butchered, and get his assurance that, since he had long since shot up a funeral cortège of Muhammad Ali's family, wounding Muhammad Ali and killing a number of his clan, he considered the score settled. Hence, he would not feel honor-bound to attack Muhammad Ali if he returned to the foot of the cliff. I took this good news back to Muhammad Ali, who opened his shirt, showed me the scar on his chest, bragged that he had been shot but not killed, yet emphasized that if he ever laid eyes on the son of Ahmad Isma'il again, he would kill him on the spot. As a result of this display of a braggadocio's fearlessness, he could be persuaded to go to the cliff, camouflaged in my clothes, in a government jeep, with me sitting on the "bullets" side facing the village and him on the safer cliff side, at dusk in Ramadan, when all Muslims are at home eating their fill after fasting throughout the daylight hours.[6]

The precise circumstances of the discovery of the Nag Hammadi library are still debated among scholars, and the debate is likely to continue into the future. However the codices of the Nag Hammadi library may have been uncovered on that eventful day in or around 1945, the discoverers could not have imagined the impact these texts, especially the Gospel of Thomas (Codex II,2), would have on our understanding of early Christianity and the world of antiquity and late antiquity.

The Gospel of Thomas is a sayings gospel. There is very little narrative in the Gospel of Thomas, and although Jesus does not do much in the Gospel of Thomas, he says a great deal (the sayings

6. Robinson, "Nag Hammadi: The First Fifty Years," 80.

of Jesus in the Gospel of Thomas are numbered, conventionally, at 114 sayings). Unlike the ways in which Jesus is portrayed in the New Testament gospels, Jesus in the Gospel of Thomas performs no physical miracles, reveals no fulfillment of prophecy, announces no apocalyptic kingdom of God about to disrupt the world order, dies for no one's sins, and does not rise physically from the dead on the third day.[7] He lives, to be sure, but he lives through his words and sayings, and as the Gospel of Thomas says in the first saying, "Whoever discovers what these sayings mean will not taste death." Jesus does not pull rank in the Gospel of Thomas; he is, as Stephen Patterson has put it, just Jesus.[8] Few Christological titles are applied to Jesus in the Gospel of Thomas, and if he is said to be a child of humanity (or, son of man) and a living one, these same titles and epithets are applied to other people of knowledge and insight.

In short, the Gospel of Thomas does not proclaim a gospel of the cross, like the New Testament gospels, but rather a gospel of wisdom; and if it recalls any early Christian text, it calls to mind the synoptic sayings gospel Q. The Gospel of Thomas, however, offers a more mystical—even gnosticizing—presentation of sayings of Jesus, and in the Gospel of Thomas the sayings are said to be hidden or secret sayings. The gospel opens, in its prologue, "These are the hidden sayings the living Jesus spoke and Judas Thomas the Twin recorded," and so Judas Thomas the Twin, perhaps thought to be the twin brother of Jesus, is the one who writes everything down. Far from being the doubting Thomas of the Gospel of John, the Thomas of the Gospel of Thomas, of all people, knows the mind of his brother. The reader or hearer of the gospel is invited to interact with these sayings of Jesus, to seek and find and uncover the meaning through the hiddenness of the text—to find the meaning or interpretation, the *hermeneia*, as saying 1 puts it. Saying 2 outlines the process whereby one comes to wisdom and knowledge: Jesus says, "Seek and do not stop seeking until you find. When you find, you will be troubled. When you are troubled,

---

7. Cf. Meyer, *The Gospel of Thomas: The Hidden Sayings of Jesus*, 6–7.

8. Cf. Patterson, Robinson, and Bethge, *The Fifth Gospel* (2nd ed.), 36.

you will marvel and reign over all." In other words, according to the Gospel of Thomas, the encounter with the hidden sayings of Jesus brings true salvation in the reign of God.

Gospel of Thomas saying 3 offers insight into precisely where the kingdom or reign of God is. Jesus tells a little joke and says,

> If your leaders tell you, "Look, the kingdom is in heaven," then the birds of heaven will precede you. If they say to you, "It's in the sea," then the fish will precede you. Rather, the kingdom is inside you and it is outside you. When you know yourselves, then you will be known, and you will understand that you are children of the living Father. But if you do not know yourselves, then you dwell in poverty and you are poverty.

The kingdom of God, Jesus says in the Gospel of Thomas, is not simply in heaven or in Hades. It is without and within, and it is achieved through true knowledge of self, the self that is within.

Saying 108 of the Gospel of Thomas completes this mystical thought of the reign of God within with reference to one's relationship with Jesus. In this saying Jesus declares, "Whoever drinks from my mouth will become like me. I myself shall become that person, and the hidden things will be revealed to that one." Finally, according to the Gospel of Thomas, one becomes Christ and Christ becomes that person, and in this way what is hidden is revealed. Or, as the Gospel of Philip, the text that follows the Gospel of Thomas in Codex II of the Nag Hammadi library (Codex II,3), puts it, don't just become a Christian; become Christ—Christ within.

~

The Gospel of Mary was discovered in 1896 when a German scholar, Carl Reinhardt, bought the Berlin Gnostic Codex from a dealer from Akhmim, in central Egypt.[9] As with the Gospel of

---

9. On the story of the discovery of the Berlin Gnostic Codex, cf. King, *The Gospel of Mary of Magdala*, 7–12; Meyer, *The Gnostic Discoveries*, 19–20; Meyer, *The Nag Hammadi Scriptures*, 1–5; Waldstein and Wisse, *The Apocryphon of John*, 2–3.

Thomas, Greek fragments of the Gospel of Mary were also found in the ancient rubbish heap at Oxyrhynchus. The dealer claimed that what is now known as the Berlin Codex had been discovered with feathers covering it in a recessed place in a wall; Carl Schmidt, the first editor of the codex, suspected that it may have come from a cemetery near Akhmim. Carl Schmidt published the last text of the codex—the Act of Peter (Berlin Gnostic Codex 4)—in 1903, and he was prepared to publish this entire papyrus book in 1912, but curses fit for the legendary stories of Egyptian magic began to afflict the lives of those working on the codex. A water pipe burst at the print shop in Leipzig and destroyed the pages being prepared for publication. World War I broke out and delayed the publication of the book. Carl Schmidt died. World War II further hindered the book's appearance. The Nag Hammadi library was discovered in 1945 and distracted scholars from work on the Berlin codex. At last, in 1955, Walter C. Till, who assumed editorial responsibility for the Berlin codex after the death of Carl Schmidt, was able to see the first three texts of the codex—the Gospel of Mary (Berlin Gnostic Codex 1), the Secret Book of John (Berlin Gnostic Codex 2), and the Wisdom of Jesus Christ (Berlin Gnostic Codex 3)—through the press; and in 1972 Hans-Martin Schenke published a second, revised edition of the Berlin Gnostic Codex.[10]

The Gospel of Mary unfortunately has been treated rather poorly by vermin and the forces of corruption in nature, and six pages are missing at the beginning of the text and four pages in the middle. In the first extant portion of the gospel, we come upon Jesus discussing, in terms that are similar to Stoic concepts, the way in which the nature of every person is restored and resolved. Jesus observes that the basic human problem in life is not the result of sin but rather of metaphysics: it is getting mixed up in what is not essentially good in the world. Jesus says, "There is no such thing as sin. You create sin when you commingle as in adultery, and that is what is called sin. That is why the good came among you, to those

---

10. Till and Schenke, *Die gnostischen Schriften des koptischen Papyrus Berolinensis 8502.*

of each nature, to restore each nature to its root" (7). Jesus goes on to summarize his word of proclamation:

> Peace be with you; receive my peace. Take care that no one deceives you by saying, "Look, here," or "Look, there." The child of humanity (the son of man) is within you. Follow that. Those who seek it will find it. Go out and preach the message of good news about the kingdom. Do not make any rules other than what I have given you, and do not lay down law, as the lawgiver has done, or you will be bound by it. (8–9)

The most remarkable statement in this remarkable passage must be the comment about the child of humanity or son of man. It is no apocalyptic figure or other external human being; the child of humanity is the inner person, the true being of a human being. That inner person is what people should follow.

This same thought is reiterated in what Mary—Mary Magdalene—has to say shortly after this in the Gospel of Mary. In the gospel Mary Magdalene takes her place as a disciple of Jesus, in what seems to be the inner circle of disciples. In the Gospel of Mary there is no inner circle of twelve people, all specified as young men, around Jesus. Mary Magdalene, and perhaps other women, are a part of that group of disciples. According to the text, when Jesus leaves, other disciples—including the young men—are weeping, and it is Mary who tries to comfort them. She stands up, greets them, and says to them, "Do not weep or be upset or in doubt, for his grace will abide with you all and protect you. Rather, we should praise his greatness, for he has prepared us and made us human" (9). Jesus will be with us, Mary proclaims, for he has humanized us by making us truly human within. As in the Gospel of Thomas, the message of salvation in the Gospel of Mary is one of a mystical realization of true being within.

Peter and Andrew like none of this, and as he does in other texts, Peter plays the gender card. He admits that Jesus loved Mary more than any other woman, but he questions whether a woman, Mary, can be taken seriously as an authority on Jesus and his message. (Dan Brown could have been reading such passages as this as he was writing his fictional novel, *The Da Vinci Code*.) Peter protests here in the Gospel of Mary, "Did he—Jesus—really speak with a woman in private without our knowledge? Should we all turn and listen to her? Did he favor her over us?" (17). Peter has his doubts on the basis of Mary's gender, but Mary does not respond with the same preoccupation with gender, and Levi points out that Peter is just a hothead. "Certainly the savior knows her well," Levi continues. "That's why he loved her more than us" (18). Mary Magdalene is the beloved disciple in the Gospel of Mary. She is the one closest to Jesus among the disciples, and she is the one who understands the mind and the message of Jesus.

❧

The Gospel of Judas was discovered in the 1970s, in Middle Egypt, in the region of al-Minya, although the precise circumstances of the discovery remain unknown.[11] The Gospel of Judas is one text among others in an ancient codex now called Codex Tchacos. According to Herbert Krosney, who has pieced together much of the story of the ancient gospel and the bound book, Codex Tchacos was found by local fellahin, or farmers, in a cave that was located at the Jabal Qarara and had been used for a Coptic burial. The cave contained, among other things, Roman glassware in baskets or papyrus or straw wrappings. Krosney writes, in *The Lost Gospel*, "The burial cave was located across the river from Maghagha, not far from the village of Qarara in what is known as Middle Egypt. The fellahin stumbled upon the cave hidden down in the rocks. Climbing down to it, they found the skeleton of a wealthy man in a shroud. Other human remains, probably members of the dead man's family, were with him in the cave. His precious books were beside him, encased in a white limestone box."[12]

---

11. On the story of the discovery of the Gospel of Judas and Codex Tchacos, cf. Krosney, *The Lost Gospel*; Meyer, *The Gospel of Judas: On a Night with Judas Iscariot*, 1–23.

12. Krosney, *The Lost Gospel*, 10.

What happened to the Gospel of Judas and Codex Tchacos thereafter is not a pretty matter. The gospel and the codex apparently were displayed, stolen, and recovered, and eventually the codex was taken to Europe, where it was shown to scholars for possible purchase. The purchase price proved to be beyond the financial reach of any of the parties viewing the texts, and the owner left without a sale. Later the Gospel of Judas and the other texts turned up in America, and for sixteen years the papyrus was locked away in a safe deposit box in Hicksville, New York, on Long Island. A safe deposit box is not the ideal place to store fragile papyrus. In the humidity of Long Island, with nothing resembling a climatized environment, the papyrus began to disintegrate. A potential buyer from the United States, Bruce Ferrini, obtained the texts for a time, and in a misguided effort to separate the papyrus pages, he put the papyrus in a freezer, thereby causing additional damage. He also had problems with cash flow, so that he was forced to surrender some of his claims to ownership of the texts. In short, on account of the greed and ineptitude of people, the lost Gospel of Judas was in danger of being lost once again.

By the time the Maecenas Foundation and the National Geographic Society were able to secure the codex for conservation and scholarly examination, the papyrus was in wretched shape. In 2001 the prominent papyrologist Rodolphe Kasser of Switzerland saw the codex, and he says he let out a cry of shock and surprise.[13] What was once a papyrus book was now a mass of fragments thrown into a box. He began to work at conserving the papyrus and placing fragment together with fragment along with another expert, Florence Darbre of the Bodmer Foundation, and later with Gregor Wurst of the University of Augsburg. And after years of painstaking effort, nothing short of a papyrological miracle occurred. The box of a thousand fragments became a book once again, with a legible Coptic copy of the Gospel of Judas.

The work of placing papyrus fragments is based on features of papyrus sheets, which are made with strips of the papyrus reed that are placed at right angles—horizontal and vertical strips—to form

13. Cf. Kasser, Meyer, and Wurst, *The Gospel of Judas* (2nd ed.), 57.

sheets of ancient paper. The individual fibers of papyrus may have anomalies, for example, darker strands or unusual characteristics, which can be traced from one fragment to another and may allow separate fragments to be connected with each other. These factors, along with observations on the profile of the edges of fragments and the sequence of letters and words on the fragments, contribute to the work of assembling fragments. The entire operation may be compared to working on a jigsaw puzzle, except that in this case many of the pieces are missing and the edges of the pieces are rough and uneven. Nonetheless, fragment may be connected to fragment, until pages and texts may be restored.

When the large and small papyrus fragments of the Gospel of Judas and the other texts in the codex were assembled, the result was a codex. Codex Tchacos is one of the earliest examples of a bound book, and this codex should add a great deal to our knowledge of the history of bookbinding. Many of the procedures employed in the construction of an ancient book like Codex Tchacos continue to be used, more or less, to the present day. In the ancient world, papyrus sheets were cut to size and folded in half, in a series of sheets, to form quires, and the quires were bound into leather covers from sheep or goats. In order to transform the resultant softback into a hardback book, scrap papyrus from the wastebasket—letters, receipts, and the like—was pasted into the cover of the codex. This scrap papyrus, called cartonnage, from the cover of Codex Tchacos may well provide dates and indications of places, and such data should help to provide accurate information about the production of Codex Tchacos.

Yet we do have a general idea of when Codex Tchacos was assembled, and we are confident that the codex is an authentic ancient manuscript.[14] There may be no papyrus that has been as thoroughly tested as the papyrus of Codex Tchacos. It has been subjected to carbon-14 dating tests, and while Florence Darbre admits that it nearly broke her heart to destroy even tiny portions of the codex in order to test its antiquity, the carbon-14 tests have yielded results that date the codex to 280 CE, plus or minus sixty

14. Cf. Kasser, Meyer, and Wurst, *The Gospel of Judas* (2nd ed.), 207–11.

years. Further, an ink test—called a TEM or transmission electron microscopy test—confirms the same range of dates for the ink, and the paleography, or handwriting style, and the religious and philosophical contents of the codex place it comfortably in the period at the end of the third century or the beginning of the fourth. Most scholars prefer to date the Coptic codex to the earlier part of the fourth century.

In 2008 more fragments of Codex Tchacos came to light.[15] Herbert Krosney has also pursued the story of these additional papyrus fragments, and the story focuses upon the figure of Bruce Ferrini. In 2008 Ferrini declared bankruptcy in Ohio, and he admitted that he had kept back papyrus fragments from the brief time he was in possession of the codex. Krosney writes of Ferrini's actions during that period, "He also left the court-supervised proceedings at lunchtime, with his lawyer, and returned to the court an hour or so later with something like a lawyer's briefcase and what appeared to be full page fragments inside."[16] The papyrus fragments turned out to be from the pages of Codex Tchacos, and a number of the fragments are from the Gospel of Judas.

Codex Tchacos is a codex copied out near the opening of the fourth century, with several texts, including the Gospel of Judas, preserved in Coptic translation.[17] The Gospel of Judas, like the other texts in the collection, was almost certainly composed in Greek sometime before the late third or early fourth century— probably quite a bit before—and subsequently translated into Coptic and copied onto the pages of the codex. The other texts in Codex Tchacos are: 1) a copy of the Letter of Peter to Philip (Codex Tchacos *1*), also known from the Nag Hammadi library (Codex VIII,*2*); 2) a text entitled James (Codex Tchacos *2*), another copy of a document referred to as the First Revelation of James and also known from the Nag Hammadi library (Codex V,*3*); and after 3) the Gospel of Judas (Codex Tchacos *3*), 4) a

15. Cf. Krosney, Meyer, and Wurst, "Preliminary Report on New Fragments of Codex Tchacos."

16. Ibid., 283.

17. Cf. Kasser, Meyer, and Wurst, *The Gospel of Judas* (2nd ed.), 10–12.

fragmentary text, previously unknown, provisionally entitled the Book of Allogenes, or the Stranger (Codex Tchacos 4), in which Jesus is depicted as a stranger in this world. 5) There must have been at least one additional text in the codex, and Gregor Wurst, who collaborated on the publication of the Gospel of Judas and Codex Tchacos, has discovered a fragment with what appears to be a page number—108—that could extend the length of the codex far beyond the current contours. Fragments with references to Hermes Trismegistus, the hero of Hermetic spirituality, have been identified by Jean-Pierre Mahé and Gregor Wurst, so that Codex Tchacos must have included a Hermetic text—apparently a Coptic translation of Corpus Hermeticum XIII (Codex Tchacos 5). But then where is the rest of Codex Tchacos? Has it disintegrated into dust? Or is it in the hands of collectors and others somewhere in the world?

Doubtless the most significant text in Codex Tchacos is the Gospel of Judas. The Gospel of Judas, so named in the manuscript itself, gives a presentation of the good news of Jesus with a mystical, gnostic emphasis. The term "gnostic" comes from the Greek word *gnosis*, which means knowledge—specifically mystical knowledge and spiritual insight. According to gnostic gospels, the true mystery of human life is that we have a spark of the divine within us, a bit of the spirit of God in our hearts, but so often we do not know it because of ignorance and distractions in our lives. Salvation for gnostics, then, means knowing ourselves, coming to a knowledge of our inner selves as the divine within, so that we may experience bliss. Obviously this sort of spirituality has much in common with forms of Hinduism, Buddhism, and other religions that have spread throughout the world, and such gnostic spirituality is fairly close to what we read in the Gospels of Thomas and Mary.

The Gospel of Judas, like the Gospels of Thomas and Mary, proclaims a way of salvation through wisdom, knowledge, and enlightenment. The gospel highlights the figure of Judas Iscariot, who is acclaimed in the Gospel of Judas as the disciple closest to Jesus who understands precisely who Jesus is. The gospel includes features that reflect Jewish and Greco-Roman—and particularly

Platonic—themes, and in the end, Jesus approaches his death, with his disciple Judas, in a way that may recall Socrates in the Phaedo. For Jesus, as for Socrates, death is not to be faced with fear but is to be anticipated with joy, for the soul or inner person is to be freed from the body of flesh.[18]

The Gospel of Judas opens with an announcement of the revelatory encounters Jesus is said to have had with the disciples and especially Judas near the end of his life: "The hidden revelatory discourse that Jesus spoke with Judas Iscariot during a period of eight days, up to three days before he celebrated Passover" (33). After this opening of the gospel, Jesus approaches his disciples as they are gathered for a holy meal, and he laughs. Jesus laughs a great deal in the Gospel of Judas, particularly, it seems, because of the foibles and absurdities of human life. Here the disciples protest against his laughter, but Jesus says that he is not laughing at them at all but at the way they take their religious rituals (in this instance, the holy meal) so seriously, as if their god demands such observance. Jesus invites the disciples to stand before him and face him, but none of them can do it, except Judas, who stands before Jesus but averts his eyes in modesty. Then Judas offers his confession of who Jesus is—the true confession, according to the Gospel of Judas. He says to Jesus, "I know who you are and where you have come from. You have come from the immortal aeon of Barbelo, and I am not worthy to utter the name of the one who has sent you" (35). To state that Jesus is from the immortal aeon or eternal realm of Barbelo is to profess that Jesus comes from the divine and is a child of God, and the name Barbelo, most likely derived from the Hebrew language, means something very much like "God in Four"—that is, God as known through the tetragrammaton, the holy and ineffable name of God in Jewish tradition, YHWH (Yahweh).[19]

18. This point has been suggested to me by Dennis MacDonald, who also recalls that there is laughter in the Phaedo just as there is laughter in the Gospel of Judas. On Platonic themes in the Gospel of Judas, see the notes to the text. On the death of Jesus and the death of Socrates, cf. the Gospel of the Redeemed in the Epilogue, below.

19. Cf. Kasser, Meyer, and Wurst, *The Gospel of Judas* (2nd ed.), 32; Harvey,

In the central portion of the Gospel of Judas, Jesus takes Judas aside and explains to him the fundamental issue in human life, as gnostic mystics conceive of it: how does the light and spirit of God come from the transcendent realm of the divine into our hearts and lives? Jesus reveals this mystery to Judas by describing the descent or devolution of the divine light into this world below from the infinite realm of God above. Jesus begins by saying to Judas, "[Come], that I may teach you about the things . . . that the human . . . will see. For there is a great and infinite aeon, whose dimensions no angelic generation could see. [In] it is the great invisible [Spirit], which no eye of an angel has seen, no thought of the mind has grasped, nor was it called by any name" (47). In a manner reminiscent of Jewish mysticism—such as we see in Jewish Kabbalah, with its tree of life and its Sefirot, or channels of divine energy emanating from Ein Sof, the infinite God—Jesus tells Judas, and the readers of the Gospel of Judas, that from the transcendent world of the divine there flow forth first one who is Self-Conceived, and then angels, messengers, attendants, aeons, luminaries, heavens, firmaments, and even an ideal image of Adamas, or Adam the first man, down to this world. This world of ours, however, with its limitations, hardships, mortality, and darkness, comes from the creative work of lower angelic beings with names appropriate for their ignorant involvement in the material world: Nebro, meaning "rebel"; Yaldabaoth, meaning "child of chaos" or something similar; and Sakla, meaning "fool"—names from the Aramaic language. In the stark contrast between the light and knowledge of God and this world of darkness and ignorance lies the human dilemma for Jesus, Judas, and all of us: the light and spirit of God come down into our hearts, but we are still trapped within an imperfect world and bodies of flesh that prevent us from realizing our true divine destiny. We need liberation.

Near the conclusion of the Gospel of Judas, after Jesus has explained everything, he turns to Judas and says, "You will exceed all of them (probably the other disciples). For you will sacrifice the man who bears me" (56). In uttering these words, Jesus announces

Irenaeus, *Libros quinque adversus haereses*, 221–22.

that Judas will turn him over to the authorities to be crucified, but he goes on to declare that the result of the sacrifice and crucifixion will be good news, news of triumph over the malevolent forces of the world. In the words of Jesus in the text, now expanded with the additional fragments, after these events leading to the crucifixion have taken place, "the ministers of the aeon have . . . , and the kings have become weak, and the generations of the angels have grieved, and those who are evil . . . the ruler, since he is overthrown. And then the image of the great generation of Adam will be magnified, for prior to heaven, earth, and the angels, that generation from the aeons exists" (57). Some of the text is lost, but we can anticipate that nothing all that good happens to the ministers of the aeon and those who are evil. Jesus, for his part, is freed of the body of flesh, and (the additional fragments now make clear) he ascends to a light cloud, enters it, and realizes his enlightened state. Judas returns to Jerusalem, and in an understated conclusion to the gospel, Judas hands over the body of Jesus to the authorities to be crucified. With this scene the Gospel of Judas concludes, and no account of the actual crucifixion is given. It is, after all, not centrally a redemptive event.

At the end of the Gospel of Judas the spiritual person of Jesus is gone, having ascended to the light above, and what Judas hands over—or betrays—is only the mortal body that once bore Jesus. Enlightened bliss is the destiny of Jesus and, by implication, also the destiny of all those who are enlightened within.

We can be assured that historians, theologians, and other scholars will be studying the Gospel of Judas for decades to come, in order to analyze its place in the history of early Christianity. The present Coptic translation of the Gospel of Judas was prepared, as we have noted, around 300 CE or shortly thereafter, but the original Gospel of Judas must have been composed in Greek in the middle part of the second century, only a few decades after the New Testament gospels were written. With its mystical message and its fascinating portrayal of Judas Iscariot, the Gospel of Judas will help scholars rewrite a part of the history of the church during the early period.

For scholars and all interested people, the Gospel of Judas raises important issues for reflection and evaluation. To begin with, the Gospel of Judas, like the Gospels of Thomas and Mary, underscores the fact that the early church was a very diverse phenomenon, with different gospels, different understandings of the good news, and different ways of believing in Jesus and following him. Frequently it has been suggested, initially in the New Testament Acts of the Apostles and more definitively by the church historian Eusebius of Caesarea, that the Christian church developed as a unified movement with a singular view of truth and orthodoxy and a common commitment to the eradication of falsehood and heresy. The Gospel of Judas, with its alternative presentation of Jesus and Judas, reminds us that the story of the church, from its earliest days, discloses a variety of manifestations of Christian thought. From the beginning, the church has been characterized by diversity, and that rich heritage of diversity continues to the present day.

The Gospel of Judas raises the issue of the nature of orthodoxy and heresy in an especially vivid way. The Gospel of Judas was referred to by its title in the writings of the heresiologist Irenaeus of Lyon around 180 CE, and he maintained that this gospel was a pernicious piece of heresy. The Gospel of Judas, in turn, throws accusations back in the faces of the leaders and members of the emerging orthodox church. This argument about who is right and who is wrong—that is, who is orthodox and who is heretical—is not only about theology and doctrine. It is a dispute with rhetorical and political overtones, and the winner in the debate is determined by who has the most convincing arguments, the most powerful voices, and the most votes as decisions are made in the life of the church. So, from an historical perspective, we may conclude that when Irenaeus and friends, who represent the thought of the emerging orthodox church and consider themselves to be thoroughly orthodox, speak of what is orthodox and what is heretical among the options in the early church, they are not just identifying orthodoxy and heresy. They are creating the categories orthodoxy and heresy.[20]

With its provocative picture of Judas Iscariot, now the close disciple of Jesus who knows who Jesus is, from a gnostic point of view, and listens to all that Jesus has to reveal, the Gospel of Judas raises questions about the image of Judas Iscariot in the New Testament gospels and other early Christian literature.[21] The more positive place of Judas in the Gospel of Judas may remind us of the hints about the character of Judas in the New Testament gospels, in spite of their eventual demonization of him. In the New Testament gospels, Judas is chosen by Jesus to be a part of the inner circle of disciples—the Twelve, in anticipation of a new Israel, with its twelve tribes—and according to the Gospel of John, Judas was entrusted with the care of the group's finances. If Judas is said to be the one dipping his bread into the sauce with Jesus at the last supper, does that mean he was understood to be sitting next to Jesus, perhaps as one of his closest friends? If Judas kissed Jesus in the garden, in a greeting between friends still practiced throughout the Middle East today, does that intimate that there were close ties between Judas and Jesus? What did Jesus have in mind when he told Judas to do what he had to do, and do it quickly?

Thus, the Gospel of Judas may provide the occasion for the reexamination of the figure of Judas Iscariot in the New Testament and other early Christian literature, with a fuller recognition of his character and the ways in which his character could be portrayed. Upon careful reexamination, the character of Judas may need to be thoroughly reassessed. This could be the time for the much-maligned disciple to be restored at the side of Jesus once again, as a close disciple of Jesus in the literary and theological tradition.[22]

---

20. Cf. King, *What Is Gnosticism?*; Marjanen, *Was There a Gnostic Religion?*; Marjanen and Luomanen, *A Companion to Second-Century Christian "Heretics"*; Williams, *Rethinking "Gnosticism"*.

21. Cf. Meyer, *Judas*.

22. Cf. Meyer, *The Gospel of Judas: On a Night with Judas Iscariot*.

❧

The discovery of the Gospel of Thomas, the Gospel of Mary, and the Gospel of Judas, along with a substantial number of other early Christian texts, provides an opportunity for a fresh look at the world of early Christianity. In these gospels divergent evaluations of the figures of disciples and interpretations of the gospel of Jesus are highlighted, and some of the maligned and marginalized disciples are redeemed.

Redemption can mean healing. It can mean forgiveness, restitution, restoration.

If Thomas is redeemed, where may be the healing? Doubting Thomas, caricatured as something of an agnostic in the New Testament Gospel of John, can at times be used to oppose traditions of Thomas Christianity that propose a more mystical, gnosticizing emphasis, such as we find in the Gospel of Thomas. The Gospel of Thomas proclaims a mystical message of good news—the good news of the wisdom and insight of the living Jesus. That this is a different formulation of the Christian gospel than the proclamation of the cross as found, variously, in Paul and the New Testament gospels, is clear. It may be the case that an acknowledgment of the Gospel of Thomas and other similar gospels may lead to an acceptance—even a celebration—of a diversity of gospels and understandings of Jesus in our own religious groups, and perhaps even an abandonment of the debates and battles about orthodoxy and heresy, truth and error, that may poison our religious interactions. Further, the Gospel of Thomas, like the Gospels of Mary and Judas, proclaims a gospel of wisdom and a theology of wisdom, and such a proclamation may provide an approach to spirituality in our day that is thoroughly viable, arguably even more viable than a gospel of the cross.

If Mary is redeemed, where may be the healing? The well-known image of Mary Magdalene as the prostitute-turned-follower-of-Jesus has inspired artists and literary figures, and the fictional tale of Mary is moving and poignant. The end result of this image of Mary, however, when combined with the image of the other main Mary in Christian tradition—the virgin Mary, the mother of Jesus—is the perpetuation of an old stereotype, that women are to be seen as either virgins or whores. That stereotype has served humanity very poorly, and the restoration of Mary Magdalene as the figure of an independent, insightful, and capable leader may provide an important way for us to address issues of discipleship and gender in our world, including the lingering gender inequities and institutionalized sexism we identify in society and religion.

If Judas is redeemed, where may be the healing? The traditional negative interpretation of Judas, which becomes more emphatically harsh as the centuries pass in the history of the church, calls to mind the place of Judas in the history of anti-Semitism. Eventually Judas Iscariot becomes a building block in the construction of the systematic hatred of anti-Semitism, and Judas himself becomes, in legend and artwork, a caricature of an evil Jew who betrays his master for money. We all realize that hatred is not easily defeated, but it may be the case that the Gospel of Judas and the figure of a redeemed Judas may provide an opportunity for Jews, Christians, Muslims, and others to come together and reconsider Judas and his relationship to anti-Semitism. This could constitute one important step in the process of addressing the anti-Semitic attitudes and other forms of intolerance and hatred that have plagued and still plague our life together.

The Gospels of Thomas, Mary, and Judas are now available to be read and studied by scholars around the world and by all of us. Lost gospels have been found, and now we may discover for ourselves how these extraordinary texts may illumine the history of religious traditions from the world of the past as well as the continuing quests for goodness, life, and light in our own world.

This book presents translations of the Gospels of Thomas, Mary, and Judas within the context of the interpretation and reinterpretation of these marginalized disciples in early Christian literature. The translations of these texts build upon previous translations I have done over the years. The translation of the Gospel of Judas is reproduced from the volume published by Cascade Books, *The Gospel of Judas: On a Night with Judas Iscariot*. The translations of the Gospels of Thomas and Mary published here have been prepared specifically for this book. My earlier translations of these gospels have been published in *The Gnostic Gospels of Jesus*, *The Gospel of Thomas: The Hidden Sayings of Jesus*, *The Gospels of Mary, Judas*, and *The Nag Hammadi Scriptures*, and, in collaboration with Willis Barnstone, *Essential Gnostic Scriptures*. All the translations of the other texts cited here are my own, unless otherwise noted.

Within the translations, square brackets indicate restorations of lacunae or gaps in the text, and dots indicate lacunae that cannot be restored with any particular confidence (for the Gospel of Judas, three dots for a lacuna of a line or less and six dots for a lacuna of more than a line). Occasionally pointed brackets are used to indicate the correction of a scribal omission or a scribal mistake. For the Gospel of Thomas, boldfaced numbers indicate the numbers traditionally assigned by scholars to the sayings of the text. For the Gospels of Mary and Judas, boldfaced numbers indicate the page numbers of the codex. Introductions to the translations place the texts in the broader world of traditions about the figures of Thomas, Mary Magdalene, and Judas Iscariot. Notes are added to clarify the meaning of passages and suggest parallels to readings in the texts. In an epilogue I offer a gospel text under the title "Gospel of the Redeemed: Draft Chapters in a Gospel of Wisdom, with Restored Disciples," as an attempt to show how the gospel story may read as a gospel of wisdom with very different visions of Thomas, Mary Magdalene, and Judas Iscariot. The book concludes with a fairly extensive bibliography.

2

THOMAS

Introduction

In the New Testament, Thomas assumes his place as one of the disciples of Jesus, though not a particularly prominent one in the synoptic gospels.[1] In the lists of the traditional twelve disciples—in Mark 3:16–19; Matthew 10:2–4; Luke 6:14–16; and Acts 1:13—Thomas settles into the middle of the lists, neither taking the lead with Peter, James, and John, nor taking up the rear with Judas Iscariot. Thereafter Thomas is not mentioned again in the synoptics. The situation is markedly different in the Gospel of John, where specific attention is called to Thomas in three scenes. In John 11, in the context of the story of the death and the raising of Lazarus, Jesus discusses the fact that Lazarus has fallen asleep, and the rather dimwitted disciples think that Jesus meant Lazarus was taking a nap. When Jesus clarifies his meaning and explains that he is talking about death, Thomas says to the others, "Let's also go, so that we may die with him," namely Jesus (11:16). In John 14, as Jesus is discoursing about what and where the way of Jesus is, Thomas

1. For a fuller discussion of the ancient texts presented here, cf. Meyer, *The Gospel of Thomas: The Hidden Sayings of Jesus*; Meyer, *Nag Hammadi Scriptures*; Patterson, *The Gospel of Thomas and Jesus*; Patterson, Robinson, and Bethge, *The Fifth Gospel*; Robinson, "LOGOI SOPHON: On the Gattung of Q."

misses the point entirely, and he blurts out, "Master, we do not know where you're going, so how can we know the way?" (14:5). To this Jesus replies, famously, with an aretalogical self-predication, "I am the way, the truth, and the life" (14:6). And in John 20, in an account of post-resurrection appearances of Jesus, Thomas earns his title of "doubting Thomas" by declaring, "Unless I see the nail wounds in his hands, and put my finger on the nail mark, and place my hand into his side, I won't believe" (20:25). Later, when Jesus appears, he invites Thomas to look at his wounds and touch them, and to believe. Thomas does so, declaring, "My master and my God," and Jesus responds, "Have you believed because you've seen me? Blessings on those who believe without seeing" (20:29).

The final scene with Thomas in the Gospel of John is memorable, and it sets Thomas up, near the end of the gospel, so that Jesus can deliver his important one-liner. In the scene Thomas is made to believe in the crucified and risen Christ, belatedly, by seeing and touching. The hearers and readers of the gospel who come to faith, conversely, will be unable to see or touch, and for their faith, their nearly blind faith, they are pronounced blessed. The author of the Gospel of John creates the scene with Thomas and his doubts as a literary device in order to allow Jesus to congratulate future believers in the cross and resurrection, and in the fictionalized narrative Thomas is left, with his uncertainties, hanging onto the bloody hands and side of Jesus, and only then coming to faith.

The proclamation of the Gospel of John is rooted in the world of Syrian Christianity, as is another early text that features Thomas, the Gospel of Thomas. Thomas is front and center in the Gospel of Thomas, and in this text he has no doubts. He is the twin brother of Jesus, and he is the one who records the hidden sayings of Jesus within the gospel (prologue). When Jesus asks the disciples to compare him to someone or something, Simon Peter and Matthew give weak responses, but Thomas says, "Teacher, my mouth is utterly incapable of saying what you are like," and Jesus takes Thomas aside and speaks three words, three sayings—words or sayings that are potent in their implications but remain hidden (saying 13). In the Gospel of Thomas, as in other texts of Syrian background, including Syriac versions of the Gospel of John, Thomas is called Judas Thomas, or Didymos Judas Thomas. Technically Thomas is not a name but a nickname that means "Twin" in Aramaic and Syriac, and Didymos means the same thing in Greek. In Syrian traditions, Judas Thomas, or Judas the Twin, was considered the twin of Jesus, who in New Testament discussions of his family is said to have a brother named Judas. Judas, or Judah, Yehuda, was a common name in ancient Israel, a name derived from Judah or Yehuda son of Jacob of Hebrew fame, and several individuals named Judas are known from the New Testament and early Christian literature, including Judas Iscariot. In the Gospel of Thomas, Judas Thomas the Twin is designated the recorder, even the guarantor, of the sayings of Jesus preserved in the gospel. As a sayings gospel, the Gospel of Thomas presents these sayings of Jesus as words of wisdom that can liberate and save. According to the first saying, "Whoever finds the interpretation of these sayings will not taste death." The point of the gospel does not involve embracing the hands and the side of the crucified Jesus. Rather, the Gospel of Thomas invites the reader to encounter the sayings of Jesus, the living Jesus who lives in his sayings, and thus to come to wisdom and knowledge.

The nature of the encounter with Jesus and his sayings in the Gospel of Thomas seems to be interactive. In his study titled *The Gospel of Thomas*, Richard Valantasis calls the theology of the gospel "a performative theology," and he proposes that the gospel looks for readers or hearers to encounter the hidden sayings creatively and find their own interpretive meaning. The theological meaning of the sayings, then, "emerges from the readers' and the hearers' responses to the sayings and their sequence and their variety."[2] He continues,

> The readers and the interpreters of sayings . . . construct
> their own narrative and theology linking the individual
> saying into a cohesive text. In that strategy, the readers
> mirror the activity of the recorder of the sayings who has
> already constructed a meaningful meta-text of collected
> individual sayings. The recorder has also constructed

2. Valantasis, *The Gospel of Thomas*, 7.

a voice for the meta-text and described that voice as
the "living Jesus" whose speaking conveys life, meaning, knowledge, immortality, and all the riches of the
Kingdom.[3]

The Jesus of the Gospel of Thomas speaks in an elusive manner, with hidden sayings and cryptic utterances, and he invites
those who hear his sayings to interact with him, find meaning, and
live. He instructs hearers to seek and find. To that extent the Jesus
of Thomas may not be so different from the Jesus of Q and the New
Testament synoptic gospels. And the Jesus of Thomas may not be
so different from the Buddha in Theravada Buddhism. Like the
Buddha, Jesus points the way, but it is up to those who hear and
follow to labor at the interpretive task.

A similar preoccupation with Jesus as a sage may be found in
two other texts connected to Thomas in the Nag Hammadi library,
the Book of Thomas (Codex II,7) and the Dialogue of the Savior
(Codex III,5). The Book of Thomas opens with words recalling the
incipit, or prologue, of the Gospel of Thomas: "The hidden sayings
that the savior spoke to Judas Thomas, which I, Mathias, in turn
recorded. I was walking, listening to them speak with each other"
(138). As the text unfolds, Jesus calls Judas Thomas his "twin and
true friend," and his brother, and he declares that Thomas has
come to knowledge of himself. (Hans-Martin Schenke speculates
that the reference to Thomas as Jesus' "true friend" actually may
come from the Greek for "the one whom Jesus truly loved."[4]) In the
discussion that transpires between Jesus and Thomas, many of the
same words and themes found in the Gospel of Thomas are also to
be noted in the Book of Thomas. To be sure, the Gospel of Thomas

---

3. Ibid., 196.

4. Schenke argues (in "The Function and Background of the Beloved
Disciple in the Gospel of John," 123) that the Coptic clause in the Book of
Thomas, "You are my twin and my true friend," may be translated back into
Greek (omitting the reference to the twin) as *su ei . . . ho philos mou ho alethi-
nos*, which Schenke rephrases in Johannine syntax and style as *su ei hon philo
alethos* (in the 2nd person singular), or *autos estin hon ephilei alethos ho Iesous*
(in the 3rd person singular), which brings us very close to Johannine statements about the beloved disciple.

proclaims the value of the spiritual life over the life of the flesh, but the Book of Thomas goes much farther in an ascetical direction as it rages against the fire of passion that characterizes life in the flesh. The Gospel of Thomas concludes with a harsh statement against Mary from the apostle Peter along with what must be a symbolic statement about the female becoming male (saying 114), but the Book of Thomas has Jesus denounce the ways of the female in no uncertain terms, with a word of shame and woe: "Shame on you who love intercourse and filthy association with the female" (144).

A figure named Judas also appears in the Dialogue of the Savior, and it is most likely that this figure is thought to be Judas Thomas, since the Dialogue of the Savior is a text that features the words and wisdom of Jesus and contains close parallels to the Gospel of Thomas. Conceivably the Judas of the Dialogue of the Savior could be understood to be Judas Iscariot, who is the leading disciple of the Gospel of Judas, but this identification is much less likely. In the Dialogue of the Savior, three disciples are mentioned as partners in dialogue with Jesus, Matthew, Mary (Magdalene), and Judas, and the topics that emerge in the discussion—knowledge and the inner life, spirit and body, light and darkness, life and death—are reminiscent of passages in the Thomas literature and gnostic texts. As in the Gospel of Thomas and the Book of Thomas, the Dialogue of the Savior raises the issue of the female, and Judas himself comments, "The works of the [female] will perish" (145). Still, throughout the text Mary Magdalene is pictured in discussion with Jesus, and she is acclaimed for her knowledge and understanding.

The person of Thomas appears throughout Syriac literature and accounts of Syrian Christianity.[5] Thomas plays a part in the story of King Abgar of Edessa, and according to Eusebius of Caesarea and others, Thomas became the apostle to the Parthians. He is linked to a Revelation, or Apocalypse, of Thomas, as well as the Acts of Thomas, in which he is the main actor and the missionary to India. In the Acts of Thomas, Didymos Judas Thomas is, again,

5. Cf. Drijvers, "The Acts of Thomas"; Klijn, *The Acts of Thomas*; Meyer, *The Nag Hammadi Scriptures*, 779–83.

the twin brother of Jesus, and within the account are statements that bring to mind sayings in the Gospel of Thomas. Like Thomas in the Gospel of Thomas, here Judas Thomas cannot comprehend the mystery of Jesus, and he too is told three words. At the opening of the text, Thomas is chosen to be the apostle to India, and when he is reluctant to go, Jesus offers Thomas as his slave, to be sent as a carpenter for King Gundaphoros, and Thomas can only concede that Jesus is indeed his lord and master. In the narrative of the Acts of Thomas, Thomas heads to India, all the while performing miracles and mighty deeds and urging the people to avoid the life of sexuality, marriage, and the flesh. Not everyone in India receives this message in a positive way, and finally Thomas is martyred in India; but even so, at the end of this fantastic tale, dust from his pious apostolic bones can bring healing.

The legend of Thomas goes on. It is said that after his martyrdom, his bones were brought back to Edessa; and the travel journal of the Christian pilgrim Egeria reports that on her visit to Edessa in the fourth century she was able to view the bones. To the present day, the legacy of St. Thomas as apostle to India continues, and the Saint Thomas Christians, or Syrian Christians, remain a part of Indian religious life today.

The Gospel of Thomas is preserved in Coptic as the second tractate in Codex II of the Nag Hammadi library. Greek fragments of versions of the Gospel of Thomas have been identified among the Oxyrhynchus papyri as Papyrus Oxyrhynchus 1, 654, and 655, and quotations from the Gospel of Thomas are to be found in Hippolytus of Rome, *Refutatio omnium haeresium* (*Refutation of All Heresies*) 5.7.20 and 5.8.32. All of these texts are translated below. The Gospel of Thomas was almost certainly composed in Greek, and a good case can be made for a date of composition in the second century, perhaps the early second century, with some sayings and portions of sayings in the collection being even older. A date of composition for some version of the Gospel of Thomas in the latter part of the first century is not implausible.[6] The place of composition is most likely in Syria, perhaps at Edessa, where Thomas was revered. The Gospel of Thomas, along with the Acts of Thomas, was accepted as sacred literature by the Manichaeans, and Mani himself developed the concept of the twin as spiritual alter ego.[7] In the world of Islam, Abu Hamid Muhammad al-Ghazali, in his book *Ihya' 'ulum al-din* (*The Revival of the Religious Sciences*), cites numerous sayings of prophet 'Isa, and among them are sayings close to those in the Gospel of Thomas. Other Islamic sources do the same.[8] The sayings within the Gospel of Thomas include many that recall sayings of Jesus in the sayings gospel Q, and a number of sayings are given in forms that appear to be earlier than the forms of the same sayings in the New Testament gospels.[9] Many scholars come to the conclusion that the Gospel of Thomas is best considered to be a gospel essentially independent of the synoptic gospels, and that it is a primary source for the Jesus tradition.

༄

Additional Reading: Barnstone and Meyer, *The Gnostic Bible*; Davies, *The Gospel of Thomas and Christian Wisdom*; DeConick, *The Original Gospel of Thomas*; Drijvers, "The Acts of Thomas"; Hedrick, *Unlocking the Secrets of the Gospel according to Thomas*; Khalidi, *The Muslim Jesus*; Klijn, *The Acts of Thomas*; Kloppenborg, Meyer, Patterson, and Steinhauser, *Q–Thomas Reader*; Layton, *The Gnostic Scriptures*; Layton, *Nag Hammadi Codex II*; Meyer, *The Gospel of Thomas: The Hidden Sayings of Jesus*; Meyer, *The Nag Hammadi Scriptures*; Meyer, *The Unknown Sayings of Jesus*; Meyer, "Whom Did Jesus Love Most?"; Most, *Doubting Thomas*; Pagels, *Beyond Belief*; Patterson, *The Gospel of Thomas and Jesus*; Patterson, Robinson, and Bethge, *The Fifth Gospel*; Riley, *Resurrection*

6. Cf. Patterson's comments in Patterson, Robinson, and Bethge, *The Fifth Gospel* (2nd ed.), 33–38.

7. Cf., for example, Cameron and Dewey, *The Cologne Mani Codex*.

8. Cf. Khalidi, *The Muslim Jesus*; Meyer, *The Unknown Sayings of Jesus*.

9. Cf. Kloppenborg, Meyer, Patterson, and Steinhauser, *Q–Thomas Reader*.

Reconsidered; Robinson, "LOGOI SOPHON: On the Gattung of Q"; Uro, *Thomas at the Crossroads*; Valantasis, *The Gospel of Thomas.*

Translation: The Gospel of Thomas

Prologue[1] These are the hidden sayings the living Jesus[2] spoke and Judas Thomas the Twin recorded.[3]

1 And he said, "Whoever discovers what these sayings mean[4] will not taste death."[5]

2 Jesus says,[6] "Seek and do not stop seeking until you find. When you find, you will be troubled. When you are troubled, you will marvel and reign over all."[7]

3 Jesus says, "If your leaders tell you, 'Look, the kingdom is in heaven,' then the birds of heaven will precede you. If they say to you, 'It's in the sea,'[8] then the fish will precede you. Rather, the kingdom is inside you and it is outside you.[9]

"When you know yourselves, then you will be known, and you will understand that you are children of the living Father. But if you do not know yourselves, then you dwell in poverty and you are poverty."[10]

4 Jesus says, "A person old in days will not hesitate to ask a little child seven days old[11] about the place of life, and that person will live.[12] For many of the first will be last[13] and become a single one."

5 Jesus says, "Know what is in front of your face, and what is hidden from you will be disclosed to you.[14] For there is nothing hidden that will not be revealed."[15]

6 His disciples asked him and said to him, "Do you want us to fast? How should we pray? Should we give to charity? What diet should we observe?"[16]

Jesus says, "Do not lie and do not do what you hate,[17] because all things are disclosed before heaven.[18] For there is nothing hidden that will not be revealed, nothing covered that will remain undisclosed."[19]

7 Jesus says, "Blessings on the lion the human will eat, so that the lion becomes human. And foul[20] is the human the lion will eat, and the lion will become human."[21]

8 And he says, "Humankind[22] is like a wise fisherman who cast his net into the sea and drew it up from the sea full of small fish. Among them the wise fisherman found a fine large fish. He threw all the small fish back into the sea and with no difficulty chose the large fish.[23]

"If you have ears to hear, you should hear."[24]

9 Jesus says, "Look, the sower went out, took a handful of seeds, and scattered them. Some fell on the road, and birds came and pecked them up. Others fell on rock, and they did not take root in the soil and did not produce heads of grain. Others fell on thorns, and they choked the seeds and worms devoured them. And others fell on good soil, and it brought forth a good crop, yielding sixty per measure and one hundred twenty per measure."[25]

10 Jesus says, "I have cast fire upon the world, and look, I am watching it till it blazes."[26]

11 Jesus says, "This heaven will pass away and the one above it will pass away.[27]

"The dead are not alive and the living will not die.

"During the days when you ate what is dead, you made it alive. When you are in the light, what will you do?

"On the day when you were one, you became two. But when you become two, what will you do?"[28]

12 The disciples said to Jesus, "We know you will leave us. Who will be our leader then?"

Jesus says to them, "Wherever you are from, go to James the Just, for whose sake heaven and earth have come into being."[29]

13 Jesus said to his disciples, "Compare me to something and tell me what I am like."[30]

Simon Peter said to him, "You are like a just messenger."[31]

Matthew said to him, "You are like a wise philosopher."

Thomas said to him, "Teacher, my mouth is utterly incapable of saying what you are like."[32]

Jesus said, "I'm not your teacher. Because you have drunk, you are intoxicated from the bubbling spring I have tended."[33]

And he took him and withdrew, and spoke three sayings[34] to him.

When Thomas came back to his companions, they asked him, "What did Jesus say to you?"

Thomas said to them, "If I tell you one of the sayings he spoke to me, you will pick up rocks and stone me, and fire will come out of the rocks and consume you."[35]

14 Jesus says to them, "If you fast, you will bring sin on yourselves, and if you pray, you will be condemned, and if you give to charity, you will harm your spirits.[36]

"When you enter any region and walk through the countryside, and people welcome you, eat what they serve you and heal the sick among them.[37] For what goes into your mouth will not defile you. It is what comes out of your mouth that will defile you."[38]

15 Jesus says, "When you see one not born of woman, fall on your faces and worship. That is your Father."[39]

16 Jesus says, "People may think I have come to cast peace upon the world. They don't know that I have come to cast conflicts upon the earth—fire, sword, war. For there will be five in a house. There will be three against two and two against three, father against son and son against father, and they will stand alone."[40]

17 Jesus says, "I shall give you what no eye has seen, what no ear has heard, what no hand has touched, what has not arisen in the human heart."[41]

18 The disciples said to Jesus, "Tell us how our end will be."[42]

Jesus says, "Have you discovered the beginning and now are seeking the end? For where the beginning is the end will be. Blessings on you who stand at the beginning. You will know the end and not taste death.[43]

19 Jesus says, "Blessings on one who came into being before coming into being.[44]

"If you become my disciples and hear my sayings, these stones will serve you.[45]

"For there are five trees in paradise for you. They do not change, summer or winter, and their leaves do not fall. Whoever knows them will not taste death."[46]

20 The disciples said to Jesus, "Tell us what the kingdom of heaven is like."

HELENA COLLEGE
University of Montana
LIBRARY
1115 N.Roberts
Helena, MT 59601

He says to them, "It is like a mustard seed. <It> is the tiniest of seeds, but when it falls on prepared soil, it produces a large plant and becomes a shelter for birds of heaven."[47]

21 Mary said to Jesus, "What are your disciples like?"

He says, "They are like children[48] living in a field that is not theirs. When the owners of the field come, they will say, 'Give our field back to us.' The children take off their clothes in front of them to give it back, and they return their field to them.[49]

"So I say, if the owner of a house knows a thief is coming, he will be on guard before the thief arrives and not let the thief break into the house of his estate and steal his belongings.[50]

"You, then, be on guard against the world. Arm yourselves with great strength, or the robbers may find a way to reach you, for the trouble you expect will come.[51]

"Let someone among you understand.

"When the crop ripened, a person came quickly with sickle in hand and harvested it.[52]

"If you have ears to hear, you should hear."

22 Jesus saw babies nursing. He said to his disciples, "These nursing babies are like those who enter the kingdom."

They said to him, "Then shall we enter the kingdom as babies?"

Jesus says to them, "When you make two into one, and when you make inner like outer and outer like inner, and upper like lower, and when you make male and female into a single one, so that the male will not be male nor the female be female, when you make eyes in place of an eye, a hand in place of a hand, a foot in place of a foot, an image in place of an image, then you will enter [the kingdom]."[53]

23 Jesus says, "I shall choose you, one from a thousand and two from ten thousand, and they will stand as a single one."[54]

24 His disciples said, "Show us the place where you are, for we must seek it."

He says to them, "If you have ears, you should hear.

"There is light within a person of light, and it[55] shines on the whole world. If it doesn't shine, it is dark."[56]

25 Jesus says, "Love your brother like your soul.[57] Protect him like the pupil of your eye."[58]

26 Jesus says, "You see the speck in your brother's eye but not the beam in your own eye. When you take the beam out of your own eye, then you will see clearly to take the speck out of your brother's eye.[59]

27 "If you do not fast from the world, you will not find the kingdom. If you do not observe the Sabbath[60] as Sabbath, you will not see the Father."[61]

28 Jesus says, "I took my stand in the midst of the world, and I appeared to them in flesh.[62] I found them all drunk, yet none of them thirsty.[63] My soul ached for the children of humanity,[64] because they are blind in their hearts and do not see, for they came into the world empty and seek also to depart from the world empty. But now they are drunk. When they shake off their wine, they will repent."

29 Jesus says, "If flesh came into being because of spirit, it is a marvel, but if spirit came into being because of body, it is a marvel of marvels. Yet I marvel at how this great wealth has come to dwell in this poverty."[65]

30 Jesus says, "Where there are three deities, they are divine. Where there are two or one, I am with that one."[66]

31 Jesus says, "A prophet is not acceptable in the hometown. A doctor does not heal acquaintances."[67]

32 Jesus says, "A city built on a high hill and fortified cannot fall, nor can it be hidden."[68]

33 Jesus says, "What you will hear in your ear, in the other ear[69] proclaim from your rooftops. For no one lights a lamp and puts it under a basket, nor in a hidden place. You put it on a stand so that all who come and go will see its light."[70]

34 Jesus says, "If a blind person leads a blind person, both will fall into a hole."[71]

35 Jesus says, "You cannot enter the house of the strong and take it by force without binding the owner's hands. Then you can loot the house."[72]

36 Jesus says, "From morning to evening and from evening to morning, do not worry about what you will wear."[73]

37 His disciples said, "When will you appear to us and when shall we see you?"

Jesus says, "When you strip naked without shame and take your clothes and put them under your feet like little children and trample them, then you will see the child of the living one and you will not be afraid."[74]

38 Jesus says, "Often you wished to hear these sayings I am speaking to you, and you have no one else from whom to hear them. There will be days when you will seek me and you will not find me."[75]

39 Jesus says, "The Pharisees and the scholars have taken[76] the keys of knowledge[77] and have hidden them. They have not entered, nor have they allowed those who wish to enter to go inside.[78] You, then, be shrewd as snakes and innocent as doves."[79]

40 Jesus says, "A grapevine has been planted far from the Father. Since it is not strong, it will be pulled up by its root and perish."[80]

41 Jesus says, "Whoever has something in hand will be given more, and whoever has nothing will be deprived of even the little bit possessed."[81]

42 Jesus says, "Be passersby."[82]

43 His disciples said to him, "Who are you to say these things to us?"

"You do not know who I am from what I tell you.[83] You have become like the Jews. They love the tree but hate its fruit or love the fruit but hate the tree."[84]

44 Jesus says, "Whoever blasphemes against the Father will be forgiven, and whoever blasphemes against the son will be forgiven, but whoever blasphemes against the holy spirit will not be forgiven, either on earth or in heaven."[85]

45 Jesus says, "Grapes are not harvested from thorn bushes, nor are figs gathered from thistles. They yield no fruit. A good person brings forth good from the storehouse. A bad person brings forth evil things from the corrupt storehouse in the heart and says evil things. For from the abundance of the heart such a person brings forth evil."[86]

46 Jesus says, "From Adam to John the baptizer, among those born of women, no one is greater than John the baptizer, so that his eyes[87] should not be averted.[88] But I have said, whoever among you becomes a child will know the kingdom and become greater than John."[89]

47 Jesus says, "A person can't mount two horses or bend two bows. And a servant can't serve two masters, or the servant will honor one and offend the other.[90] No person drinks aged wine and suddenly wants to drink new wine. New wine is not poured into aged wineskins, or they may break, and aged wine is not poured into a new wineskin, or it may spoil.[91] An old patch is not sewn onto a new garment, for there would be a tear."[92]

48 Jesus says, "If two make peace with each other in one house, they will say to the mountain, 'Move,' and it will move."[93]

49 Jesus says, "Blessings on you who are alone[94] and chosen. You will find the kingdom. For you have come from it, and you will return there again."[95]

50 Jesus says, "If they say to you, 'Where have you come from?' say to them, 'We have come from the light, from the place where the light came into being by itself, established [itself], and appeared in their image.' If they say to you, 'Is it you?'[96] say, 'We are its children and the chosen of the living Father.' If they ask you, 'What is the evidence of your Father in you?' say to them, 'It is motion and rest.'"[97]

51 His disciples said to him, "When will the rest[98] for the dead take place, and when will the new world come?"

He says to them, "What you look for has come but you do not know it."[99]

52 His disciples said to him, "Twenty-four prophets[100] have spoken in Israel and they all spoke of you."

He says to them, "You have ignored the living one in your presence and have spoken of the dead."[101]

53 His disciples said to him, "Is circumcision useful or not?"

He says to them, "If it were useful, fathers would produce children already circumcised from their mothers. Rather, true circumcision in spirit is valuable in every respect."[102]

54 Jesus says, "Blessings on the poor. Yours is the kingdom of heaven."[103]

55 Jesus says, "Those who do not hate their father and mother cannot be my disciples, and those who do not hate their brothers and sisters and bear the cross[104] as I do will not be worthy of me."[105]

56 Jesus says, "Whoever has come to know the world has discovered a carcass, and whoever has discovered a carcass, of that person the world is not worthy."[106]

57 Jesus says, "The kingdom of the Father is like someone who had [good] seed. His enemy came at night and sowed weeds among the good seed. The person did not let them pull up the weeds but said to him, 'No, or you might go to pull up the weeds and pull up the wheat along with them.' For on harvest day the weeds will stand out and will be pulled up and burned."[107]

58 Jesus says, "Blessings on the person who has labored[108] and found life."[109]

59 Jesus says, "Look to the living one as long as you live, or you may die and then try to see the living one, and you will not be able to see."[110]

60 <He saw>[111] a Samaritan carrying a lamb as he was going to Judea.

He said to his disciples, "That person is carrying the lamb around."[112]

They said to him, "Then he may kill it and eat it."

He says to them, "He will not eat it while it is alive but only after he has killed it and it has become a carcass."

They said, "Otherwise he cannot do it."

He says to them, "So with you. Seek for yourselves a place for rest or you may become a carcass and be eaten."[113]

61 Jesus says, "Two will rest on a couch.[114] One will die, one will live."[115]

Salome said, "Who are you, mister? You have climbed onto my couch and eaten from my table as if you are from someone."[116]

Jesus said to her, "I am one who comes from what is whole. I was given from the things of my Father."[117]

"I am your disciple."

"For this reason I say, if you are <whole>,[118] you will be filled with light,[119] but if you are divided, you will be filled with darkness."

62 Jesus says, "I disclose my mysteries to those [who are worthy] of [my] mysteries.[120] Do not let your left hand know what your right hand is doing."[121]

63 Jesus says, "There was a rich man who was very wealthy. He said, 'I shall invest my money so that I may sow, reap, plant, and fill my storehouses with produce. Then I'll lack nothing.' This is what he was thinking in his heart, but that very night he died.[122]

"If you have ears, you should hear."

64 Jesus says, "A person was receiving guests. When he prepared the dinner, he sent his servant to invite the guests.

"The servant went to the first and said, 'My master invites you.'

"That person said, 'Some merchants owe me money. They are coming tonight. I must go and give them instructions. Please excuse me from dinner.'

"The servant went to another and said, 'My master has invited you.'

"He said to the servant, 'I have bought a house and I've been called away for a day. I have no time.'

"The servant went to another and said, 'My master invites you.'

"He said to the servant, 'My friend is to be married and I am to arrange the banquet. I can't come. Please excuse me from dinner.'

"The servant went to another and said, 'My master invites you.'

"He said to the servant, 'I have bought an estate and I am going to collect rent. I can't come. Please excuse me.'

"The servant returned and said to his master, 'Those whom you invited to dinner have asked to be excused.'

"The master said to his servant, 'Go out on the streets and bring back whomever you find for dinner.'[123]

"Buyers and merchants [will] not enter the places of my Father."[124]

65 He says, "A [usurer][125] owned a vineyard and rented it to some tenant farmers to work it, and from them he would collect its produce. He sent his servant so that the farmers would give the servant the produce of the vineyard. They seized, beat, and nearly killed his servant, and the servant returned and told his master. His master said, 'Perhaps he did not know them.'[126] He sent another servant, and the farmers beat that one as well. Then the master sent his son and said, 'Perhaps they will show my son some respect.' Since the farmers knew the son was the heir to the vineyard, they seized him and killed him.[127]

"If you have ears, you should hear."

66 Jesus says, "Show me the stone the builders rejected. That is the cornerstone."[128]

67 Jesus says, "Whoever knows everything but lacks within lacks everything."[129]

68 Jesus says, "Blessings on you when you are hated and persecuted, and no place will be found, wherever you are persecuted."[130]

69 Jesus says, "Blessings on you who have been persecuted in your hearts. It is you who truly know the Father.[131] Blessings on you who are hungry, that the stomach of someone in want may be filled."[132]

70 Jesus says, "If you bring forth what is within you, what you have will save you. If you do not have that within you, what you do not have within you [will] kill you."[133]

71 Jesus says, "I shall destroy [this] house and no one will be able to build it [again]."[134]

72 A [person said] to him, "Tell my brothers to divide my father's possessions with me."

He says to the person, "Mister, who made me a divider?"

He turned to his disciples and said to them, "I'm not a divider, am I?"[135]

73 Jesus says, "The harvest is large but the workers are few. Beg the master to send out workers to the harvest."[136]

74 Someone said,[137] "Master, there are many around the drinking trough, but there is nothing[138] in the <well>."[139]

75 Jesus says, "There are many standing at the door, but those who are alone[140] will enter the wedding chamber."[141]

76 Jesus says, "The kingdom of the Father is like a merchant who owned a supply of merchandise and then found a pearl. The merchant was smart. He sold his goods and bought the single pearl for himself.[142] So with you. Seek his treasure that is unfailing and enduring, where no moth comes to devour and no worm destroys."[143]

77 Jesus says, "I am the light over all things.[144] I am all. From me all has come forth, to me all has reached.[145] Split a piece of wood. I am there. Lift up the stone and you will find me there."[146]

78 Jesus says, "Why have you come out to the countryside? To see a reed shaken by the wind? Or to see a person dressed in soft clothes, [like your] rulers and your powerful people? They are dressed in soft clothes and cannot understand truth."[147]

79 A woman in the crowd said to him, "Blessings on the womb that bore you and the breasts that fed you."[148]

He says to [her], "Blessings on those who have heard the word of the Father and have truly kept it.[149] For days will come when you will say, 'Blessings on the womb that has not conceived and the breasts that have not given milk.'"[150]

80 Jesus says, "Whoever has come to know the world has discovered the body, and whoever has discovered the body, of that person the world is not worthy."[151]

81 Jesus says, "Let a person of wealth reign, and let a person of power renounce it."[152]

82 Jesus says, "Whoever is near me is near fire, and whoever is far from me is far from the kingdom."[153]

83 Jesus says, "Images are visible to people, but the light within them is hidden in the image of the Father's light. He will be disclosed, but his image is hidden by his light."

84 Jesus says, "When you see your likeness, you are happy. But when you see your images that came into being before you and neither die nor become visible, how much you will bear!"[154]

85 Jesus says, "Adam came from great power[155] and great wealth, but he was not worthy of you. Had he been worthy, [he would] not [have tasted] death."

86 Jesus says, "[Foxes have] their dens and birds have their nests, but the child of humanity[156] has no place to lay his head and rest."[157]

87 Jesus says, "Wretched is the body that depends on a body, and wretched is the soul that depends on both."[158]

88 Jesus says, "The messengers[159] and the prophets will come to you and give you what is yours. You give them what you have and say to yourselves, 'When will they come and take what is theirs?'"[160]

89 Jesus says, "Why do you wash the outside of the cup? Don't you understand that the one who made the inside is the same one who made the outside?"[161]

90 Jesus says, "Come to me, for my yoke is easy and my mastery gentle, and you will find rest for yourselves."[162]

91 They said to him, "Tell us who you are so we may believe in you."

He says to them, "You examine the face of heaven and earth, but you have not come to know who is in your presence, and you do not know how to examine this moment."[163]

92 Jesus says, "Seek and you will find.[164] In the past I did not tell you the things about which you asked me. Now I am willing to tell you, but you are not seeking them."[165]

93 "Do not give what is holy to dogs. They might throw them on the manure pile. Do not throw pearls [to] swine. They might make [mud] (?) of it."[166]

94 Jesus [says], "One who seeks will find. For [one who knocks] it will be opened."[167]

95 [Jesus says], "If you have money, do not lend it at interest. Give [it] to someone from whom you will not get it back."[168]

96 Jesus [says], "The kingdom of the Father is like [a] woman. She took a little yeast, [hid] it in dough, and made large loaves of bread.[169]

"If you have ears, you should hear."

97 Jesus says, "The kingdom of the [Father] is like a woman carrying a [jar] full of meal. While she was walking along [a] distant road, the handle of the jar broke and the meal spilled behind her [along] the road. She did not know it. She noticed no problem. When she reached her house, she put the jar down and found it was empty."[170]

98 Jesus says, "The kingdom of the Father is like a person who wanted to put a powerful person to death. While at home he drew his sword and thrust it into the wall to find out whether his hand would go in. Then he killed the powerful person."[171]

99 The disciples said to him, "Your brothers and your mother are standing outside."

He says to them, "Those here who do the will of my Father are my brothers and my mother. They are the ones who will enter the kingdom of my Father."[172]

100 They showed Jesus a gold coin and said to him, "Caesar's people demand taxes from us."

He says to them, "Give Caesar the things that are Caesar's, give God the things that are God's, and give me what is mine.[173]

101 "Those who do not hate their [father] and mother as I do cannot be my [disciples], and those who do [not] love their [father and] mother as I do cannot be my [disciples]. For my mother [gave me falsehood (?)],[174] but my true [mother][175] gave me life."[176]

102 Jesus says, "Shame on the Pharisees. They are like a dog sleeping in the cattle manger. It neither eats nor [lets] the cattle eat."[177]

103 Jesus says, "Blessings on you if you know at what point[178] the robbers will enter, so that [you] may wake up, rouse your estate, and arm yourself before they break in."[179]

104 They said to Jesus, "Come, let's pray today and fast."

Jesus says, "What sin have I committed, or how have I been undone? When the bridegroom leaves the wedding chamber, then let people fast and pray."[180]

105 Jesus says, "Whoever knows the father and the mother will be called the child of a whore."[181]

106 Jesus says, "When you make two into one, you will become children of humanity. When you say, 'Mountain, move,' it will move."[182]

107 Jesus says, "The kingdom is like a shepherd who had a hundred sheep. One of them, the largest, went astray. He left the ninety-nine and searched for the one until he found it. After he had gone to this trouble, he said to the sheep, 'I love you more than the ninety-nine.'"[183]

108 Jesus says, "Whoever drinks from my mouth will become like me. I myself shall become that person, and the hidden things will be revealed to that one."[184]

109 Jesus says, "The kingdom is like a person who had a treasure hidden in his field. He did not know it, and [when] he died,[185] he left it to his [son]. The son [did] not know about it. He took over the field and sold it. The buyer went plowing, [discovered] the treasure, and began to lend money at interest to whomever he wished."[186]

110 Jesus says, "Let someone who has found the world and become wealthy renounce the world."[187]

111 Jesus says, "The heavens and the earth will roll up in your presence, and whoever is living from the living one will not see death."[188]

Doesn't Jesus say, "Whoever has found oneself, of that person the world is not worthy"?[189]

112 Jesus says, "Shame on the flesh that depends on the soul. Shame on the soul that depends on the flesh."[190]

113 His disciples said to him, "When will the kingdom come?"

"It will not come by watching for it. It will not be said, 'Look, here,' or 'Look, there.' The kingdom of the Father is spread out upon the earth and people do not see it."[191]

114 Simon Peter said to them, "Mary should leave us, for females are not worthy of life."

Jesus says, "Look, I shall guide her to make her male, so that she too may become a living spirit resembling you males. For every female who makes herself male will enter the kingdom of heaven."[192]

The Gospel according to Thomas

🐦

Translation: The Greek Gospel of Thomas

Papyrus Oxyrhynchus 654

Prologue These are the [hidden] sayings the living Jesus spoke [and Judas, who is] also Thomas, [recorded].

1 And he said, "[Whoever discovers what] these sayings [mean] will not taste [death]."

2 [Jesus says, "Seek] and do not stop [seeking until] you find. When you find, [you will be astonished, and having been] astonished, you will reign, and [having reigned], you will [rest]."

3 Jesus says, "[If] your leaders [tell you, 'Look], the kingdom is in heaven,' the birds of [heaven will precede you. If they say] it's under the earth, the fish [will enter, and will precede] you. The [kingdom of God] is inside [and outside] you. [Whoever of you] knows [yourself] will find this.

"[And when you] know yourselves, [you will understand that] you are [children] of the [living] Father. [But if] you do [not] know yourselves, [you are] in [poverty] and you are [poverty]."

4 [Jesus says], "A [person old in] days will not hesitate to ask a [little child seven] days old about the place of [life, and] that person will [live]. For many of the [first] will be [last and] the last first, and they [will become one]."

5 Jesus says, "[Know what is before] your face, and [what is hidden] from you will be disclosed [to you. For] there [is nothing] hidden that [will] not [become] apparent, and nothing buried that [will not be raised]."

6 [His disciples] ask him and [say], "How [should we] fast? [How should] we [pray]? How [should we give to charity]? What [diet] should [we] observe?"

Jesus says, "[Do not lie and] do not do [what] you [hate, because all things are disclosed before] truth. [For there is nothing] hidden [that will not be apparent].

7 . . . "Blessings on [the lion a human eats, and the] lion will be [human. And cursed is the human a lion eats] . . ."

Papyrus Oxyrhynchus 655

24 ". . . There is [light within a person] of light, and [it shines on the whole] world. [If it doesn't shine, then] it is [dark].

Papyrus Oxyrhynchus 1

26 ". . . and then you will see clearly to take out the speck in your brother's eye.

27 Jesus says, "If you do not fast from the world, you will not find the kingdom of God. And if you do not observe the Sabbath as Sabbath, you will not see the Father."

28 Jesus says, "I took my stand in the midst of the world, and I appeared to them in flesh. I found them all drunk, and none of them thirsty. My soul aches for the children of humanity, because they are blind in their hearts and [do not] see . . ."

29 ". . . [comes to dwell in this] poverty."

30, 77 [Jesus says], "Where there are [three, they are without] God, and where there is only [one], I say, I am with that one.

"Lift up the stone and you will find me there. Split the piece of wood, and I am there."

31 Jesus says, "A prophet is not acceptable in the hometown, nor does a doctor perform healings on acquaintances."

32 Jesus says, "A city built on top of a high hill and fortified can neither fall nor be hidden."

33 Jesus says, "<What> you hear in one ear of yours, [proclaim] . . ."

Papyrus Oxyrhynchus 655

36 [Jesus says, "Do not worry], from morning to nightfall nor] from evening [to] morning, either [about] your [food], what [you'll] eat, [or] about [your robe], what clothing you'll wear. [You are much] better than the lilies, which do not card or [spin]. As for you, since you have no garment, what [will you put] on? Who may add to your stature? That is the one who will give your clothing to you."

37 His disciples say to him, "When will you be revealed to us and when shall we see you?"

He says, "When you strip off your clothing and are not ashamed . . . [and you will not be afraid]."

38 [Jesus says, "Often you wished to hear these sayings of mine], and [you have no one else from whom to hear them]. And [days will come when you will seek me and you will not find me]."

39 [Jesus says, "The Pharisees and the scholars] have [taken the keys] of [knowledge.¹⁹³ They themselves have] hidden [them. Neither] have [they] entered, [nor] have they [allowed those who are in the process of] entering [to enter. You, then, be shrewd] as [snakes and] innocent [as doves]."

Hippolytus of Rome, *Refutation of All Heresies* 5.7.20

4 "You who seek me will find me in children from seven years, for there, hidden in the fourteenth age,¹⁹⁴ I am revealed."

Hippolytus of Rome, *Refutation of All Heresies* 5.8.32

11 "If you ate dead things and made them alive, what will you do if you eat living things?"

Endnotes

1. Nag Hammadi Codex II,2: 32,10—51,28. For the Coptic text and the Greek fragments, cf. Layton, *Nag Hammadi Codex II*; Meyer, *The Gospel of Thomas: The Hidden Sayings of Jesus*. For another recent translation of the Gospel of Thomas, cited several times in the notes, cf. Patterson, Robinson, and Bethge, *The Fifth Gospel*. (The translation in *The Fifth Gospel* is based on that of the Berliner Arbeitskreis für koptisch-gnostische Schriften, as published in Aland, ed., *Synopsis Quattuor Evangeliorum*.) In the present translation I occasionally use pronouns in the second person instead of in the third person, as in the text itself, for stylistic reasons. For the same reasons I sometimes use the third-person plural rather than the third-person singular, as in the text itself. A limited selection of references may be given here in the notes. A substantial number of references to passages in Matthew and Luke are thought to derive from the sayings gospel Q. Most of my translations of texts referred to in the notes are taken from *The Gospel of Thomas: The Hidden Sayings of Jesus*. The translations of passages from Islamic texts are from *The Unknown Sayings of Jesus*.

2. The "living Jesus" is almost certainly not a reference to the resurrected Jesus as traditionally understood, but rather to Jesus who lives through his sayings.

3. Cf. Book of Thomas 138.

4. Here the Coptic uses a noun, *hermeneia*, "meaning" or "interpretation"; this saying may be read "Whoever discovers the interpretation of these sayings."

5. Cf. Sirach 39:1–3; John 8:51–52.

6. Or, "Jesus said," here and below. This Coptic verbal form used for the quotation formulae (*peje-*, *peja=*) can be translated with either the present or past tense. In a narrative context, where the past tense is implied, a translation into the past tense may be preferable. In the Greek Gospel of Thomas, most of the quotation formulae are given in the present tense. The use of the present tense in the Greek fragments and the English translation underscores the character of the sayings as words the living Jesus continues to speak in the present moment.

7. Cf. Book of Thomas 140–41; Gospel of the Hebrews 4a, 4b; Matthew 7:7–8; Luke 11:9–10; Wisdom of Solomon 6:12, 17–20. Dialogue of the Savior 129 offers the following as a saying of Jesus: "And I say to you, let one [who

has] power renounce [it and] repent, and let one who [knows] seek and find and rejoice." The Greek Gospel of Thomas adds, at the end of the saying, "and [having reigned], you will [rest]."

8. The Greek Gospel of Thomas reads "it's under the earth."

9. Cf. Luke 17:20–21; Gospel of Thomas 113. Also cf. Manichaean Psalm Book 160: "The kingdom of heaven, look, it's inside us, look, it's outside us. If we believe in it, we shall live in it forever."

10. The maxim *gnothi sauton*, "Know yourself," was among the inscriptions at the oracular site of Delphi in Greece. On a person knowing and being known, cf. Galatians 4:8–9; 1 Corinthians 8:1–3; 13:12.

11. This probably is meant to designate an uncircumcised child, since Jewish boys were usually circumcised on the eighth day.

12. A different version of this saying is to be read in Hippolytus of Rome, *Refutation of All Heresies* 5.7.20: "You who seek me will find me in children from seven years, for there, hidden in the fourteenth age, I am revealed" (see the Greek Gospel of Thomas). Cf. also Manichaean Psalm Book 192,2–3: "To the old people with gray hair the little children give instruction; those six years old give instruction to those sixty years old."

13. Cf. Mark 10:31; Matthew 19:30; 20:16; Luke 13:30; Barnabas 6:13.

14. Cf. a saying of Jesus in Manichaean Kephalaia 65 163.26–29: "Understand what is in front of your face, and then what is hidden from you will be disclosed to you."

15. Cf. Gospel of Thomas 6; Mark 4:22; Matthew 10:26; Luke 8:17; 12:2. The Greek Gospel of Thomas adds, "and nothing buried that [will not be raised]." A similar reference to being raised is found on a Christian burial shroud from Oxyrhynchus, dated to the fifth or sixth century.

16. These questions seem to be answered in saying 14. On the questions raised, cf. Matthew 6:1–18; *Didache* 8:1–3.

17. This is a negative formulation of the golden rule.

18. Here the Coptic Gospel of Thomas reads "heaven" (*pe*) and the Greek Gospel of Thomas reads "truth" (Greek *aletheia*, equivalent to Coptic *me*). Patterson, Robinson, and Bethge opt for a reading that emends the Coptic to read, with the Greek version, "<truth>."

19. Cf. Gospel of Thomas 5.

20. Or, "cursed."

21. This obscure saying seems to appeal to the lion as a symbol of all that is passionate and bestial. The passions may either be consumed by a person or consume a person. Cf. Plato's *Republic*, 588e–589b. The Secret Book of John portrays Yaldabaoth, the ruler of this world, as lionlike in appearance. On the saying in general, see Jackson, *The Lion Becomes Man*.

22. Or, "The human."

23. Cf. Matthew 13:47–50. In Greek literature, Babrius, Fable 4, reads as follows: "A fisherman drew in a net that he had just cast, and it happened to be full of a variety of fish. The little one among the fish fled to the bottom and slipped out of the porous mesh, but the large one was caught and was laid

stretched out in the boat. A way to be safe and clear of trouble is to be small, but seldom will you see a person large in reputation who escapes dangers."

24. The injunction to pay attention is found throughout the Gospel of Thomas and early Christian literature.

25. Cf. Mark 4:2–9; Matthew 13:3–9; Luke 8:4–8; Gospel of Judas 43–44.

26. Cf. Luke 12:49. Also cf. Pistis Sophia 141, where Jesus says, "For this reason I said to you, 'I have come to cast fire upon the earth,' that is, I have come to cleanse the sins of the whole world with fire."

27. Cf. Mark 13:31; Matthew 5:18; 24:35; Luke 16:17; 21:33.

28. This saying consists of four riddles about life in this world and beyond. A different phrasing of the third riddle appears in Hippolytus of Rome, *Refutation of All Heresies* 5.8.32: "If you ate dead things and made them alive, what will you do if you eat living things?" (see the Greek Gospel of Thomas).

29. James the Just was the brother of Jesus and the leader of the Jerusalem church up to the time of his death in 62 CE. The stories about James in the New Testament and early Christian literature make it clear that he had an outstanding reputation for piety.

30. On this saying in general, cf. Mark 8:27–33; Matthew 16:13–23; Luke 9:18–22. In the synoptic story set on the road to Caesarea Philippi, it is Peter who has the final answer; in Thomas' version, it is Thomas.

31. Or, "angel."

32. Compare the profession of Judas Iscariot in Gospel of Judas 35.

33. Jesus is the enlightened bartender who serves up wisdom. Cf. saying 108.

34. Or "three words" (Coptic *enshomt enshaje*). The three sayings or words are unknown. They may be mentioned here, without being identified, as a part of the strategy of the text to encourage the reader to interact with the sayings of Jesus in their frequently cryptic and enigmatic formulation. The reader must discover the interpretation. Three such words, however, are suggested elsewhere in early Christian literature: Kaulakau, Saulasau, Zeesar, in the Naassene Sermon, or Yao Yao Yao, the ineffable name of God.

35. Within Judaism stoning was the punishment for blasphemy.

36. These seem to be answers to the questions raised in saying 6.

37. Cf. Matthew 10:8; Luke 10:8–9; 1 Corinthians 10:27.

38. Cf. Mark 7:15; Matthew 15:11.

39. Cf. John 10:30.

40. The Coptic word translated as "alone" is *monakhos*. This word, also found in sayings 49 and 75, may indicate someone who is solitary, unique, or unmarried, or—later, in a more technical sense—it may designate one who is a monk. On the saying in general, cf. Matthew 10:34–36; Luke 12:49–53.

41. Paul may cite this saying in 1 Corinthians 2:9 as a wisdom saying in use among enthusiasts in Corinth. Versions of this saying occur elsewhere in ancient literature, including early Christian literature. Cf. Dialogue of the Savior 140; Gospel of Judas 47.

42. Cf. Mark 13:3–4; Matthew 24:3; Luke 21:7.

43. Cf. Gospel of Thomas 49.

44. Cf. Gospel of Philip 64: "Blessings on one who is before coming into being. For whoever is, was and will be." Also cf. Lactantius, *Divinae institutiones* (*Divine Institutes*) 4.8: "For we especially testify that he (Christ) was born twice, first in the spirit and afterwards in the flesh. Whence it is thus said in Jeremiah, 'Before I formed you in the womb, I knew you.' And also in the same work, 'Blessings on one who existed before being born,' which happened to no one else except Christ."

45. Perhaps cf. Gospel of Thomas 77.

46. The trees of paradise recall the trees of the Garden of Eden mentioned in Genesis 3. Five trees of paradise are also discussed in Manichaean texts and in the Islamic book of gnosis entitled *Umm al-kitab* (*Mother of Books*).

47. Cf. Mark 4:30–32; Matthew 13:31–32; Luke 13:18–19.

48. Here Patterson, Robinson, and Bethge adopt the translation "servants" (under the assumption that the Coptic *shere shem* derives from the Greek *pais*).

49. Cf. Gospel of Thomas 37.

50. Cf. Gospel of Thomas 103; Matthew 24:43; Luke 12:39.

51. Patterson, Robinson, and Bethge offer this translation: "For the necessities for which you wait (with longing) will be found." In a note they give another possibility: "For the possessions you are guarding they will find."

52. Cf. Mark 4:29; Joel 3:13.

53. Cf. Galatians 3:27–28; Gospel of the Egyptians; 2 Clement 12:2–6; Martyrdom of Peter 9; Acts of Philip 140; Gospel of Thomas 114. The reference in the Gospel of the Egyptians, for example, reads as follows: "Therefore Cassianus says, 'When Salome inquired when the things about which she had asked would be known, the master said, "When you have trampled the garment of shame, and when the two become one, and the male with the female is neither male nor female."' Now first of all, we don't have this saying in the four gospels handed down to us but rather in the (Gospel) according to the Egyptians." (On trampling garments, cf. saying 37.) The statement in the Martyrdom of Peter provides more parallels: "Concerning this the master says in a mystery, 'If you do not make what is on the right like what is on the left and what is on the left like what is on the right, and what is above like what is below, and what is behind like what is before, you will not recognize the kingdom.'" Gospel of Thomas 114 also discusses the transformation of genders, but in rather different terms.

54. Cf. Deuteronomy 32:30; Ecclesiastes 7:28; Pistis Sophia 134; Irenaeus, *Against Heresies* 1.24.6.

55. Or, "he," here and below.

56. Cf., in general, Matthew 6:22–23; Luke 11:34–36. Dialogue of the Savior 125–26 has Jesus say, "The lamp [of the] body is the mind. As long as [what is within] you is kept in order—that is, [the soul]—your bodies are [enlightened]. As long as your hearts are dark, your light, which you expect, [is far from you]."

57. Or, "your life," "yourself" (Coptic *tekpsukhe*).

58. Cf. Mark 12:31; Matthew 22:39; Luke 10:27; Leviticus 19:18.

59. Cf. Matthew 7:3–5; Luke 6:41–42.

60. Or, with Patterson, Robinson, and Bethge, "the (entire) week" (Coptic *psambaton*).

61. On fasting from the world, cf. Clement of Alexandria, *Stromateis* (*Miscellanies*) 3.15.99.4; on keeping the Sabbath always, cf. Tertullian, *Adversus Judaeos* (*Against the Jews*) 4.

62. Cf. John 1:14; 1 Timothy 3:16; also Proverbs 1:20–33 and Baruch 3:37 (on Wisdom appearing to people).

63. In gnostic and other similar texts, a person who is ignorant and devoid of knowledge frequently is said to be drunk.

64. Or, "sons of men."

65. Perhaps cf. Gospel of Thomas 7.

66. Cf. Matthew 18:19–20. Also cf. Ephraem Syrus, *Evangelii concordantis expositio* (*Exposition on the Harmony of the Gospel*) 14: "Where there is one, there also am I, or someone might be sad from lonely things, since he himself is our joy and he himself is with us. And where there are two, there also shall I be, since his mercy and grace overshadow us. And when we are three, we assemble just as in church, which is the body of Christ perfected and his image expressed." The Greek Gospel of Thomas, as reconstructed, seems to have a different version of the saying, and it is connected to a portion of Coptic Gospel of Thomas saying 77: "[Jesus says], 'Where there are [three, they are without] God, and where there is only [one], I say, I am with that one. Lift up the stone and you will find me there. Split the piece of wood, and I am there.'"

67. Cf. Mark 6:4; Matthew 13:57; Luke 4:23–24; John 4:44.

68. Cf. Matthew 5:14; 7:24–25; Luke 6:47–48.

69. "In the other ear" (Coptic *hem pkemaaje*) may be an inadvertent repetition of the previous phrase (*hem pekmaaje*, "in your ear," perhaps an instance of dittography), or the phrase may refer to another person's ear or perhaps even one's own "inner" ear. Cf. also the fragmentary version of this saying in the Greek Gospel of Thomas: "Jesus says, '<What> you hear in one ear of yours, [proclaim] . . .'"

70. Cf. Mark 4:21; Matthew 5:15; Luke 8:16; 11:33.

71. Cf. Matthew 15:14; Luke 6:39.

72. Cf. Mark 3:27; Matthew 12:29; Luke 11:21–22.

73. Cf. Matthew 6:25–34; Luke 12:22–32. The Greek Gospel of Thomas has a much longer saying: "[Jesus says, 'Do not worry], from morning to nightfall nor] from evening [to] morning, either [about] your [food], what [you'll] eat, [or] about [your robe], what clothing you'll wear. [You are much] better than the lilies, which do not card or [spin]. As for you, since you have no garment, what [will you put] on? Who may add to your stature? That is the one who will give your clothing to you.'"

74. Cf. Gospel of the Egyptians (see the note to saying 22); Gospel of Philip 75; Hippolytus, *Refutation of All Heresies* 5.8.44; especially cf. Manichaean Psalm Book 99,26–30: "The saying of Jesus the redeemer came to [me (?), as]

is appropriate: "'The vain garment of this flesh I have stripped off, and I am saved and purified; I have caused the clean feet of my soul to trample upon it confidently; with the gods that are clothed with Christ have I stood in line.'" Cf. Smith, "The Garments of Shame."

75. Cf. Matthew 13:17; Luke 10:24; John 7:33–36; Proverbs 1:23–28.

76. Or, "have received."

77. Gnosis.

78. Cf. Matthew 23:13; Luke 11:52. Also cf. al-Ghazali, *Revival of the Religious Sciences* 1.49: "Jesus said, 'Evil scholars are like a rock that has fallen at the mouth of a brook: it doesn't drink the water, nor does it let the water flow to the plants. And evil scholars are like the drainpipe of a latrine that is plastered outside but filthy inside, or like graves that are decorated outside but contain dead people's bones inside.'"

79. Cf. Matthew 10:16; Ignatius of Antioch, *To Polycarp* 2:2.

80. Cf. Matthew 15:13; John 15:5–6; Isaiah 5:1–7; Book of Thomas 144.

81. Cf. Mark 4:24–25; Matthew 13:12; 25:29; Luke 8:18; 19:26.

82. Or, "Be wanderers," or, less likely, in my estimation, "Come into being as you pass away" (the translation favored by Hedrick, *Unlocking the Secrets of the Gospel according to Thomas*, 87; Coptic *shope etetenerparage*). A parallel to this saying appears in an inscription from a mosque at Fatehpur Sikri, India: "Jesus said, 'This world is a bridge. Pass over it, but do not build your dwelling there.'" A very similar saying is found in the medieval author Petrus Alphonsi.

83. Cf. John 14:8–11.

84. Cf. Matthew 7:16, 19–20; 12:33; Luke 6:43–44.

85. Cf. Mark 3:28–29; Matthew 12:31–32; Luke 12:10.

86. Cf. Matthew 7:16–29; 12:33–35; Luke 6:43–45; James 3:12.

87. Probably the person's eyes, possibly John's.

88. This probably refers to people averting their eyes in deference or modesty. Cf. Gospel of Judas 35.

89. Cf. Matthew 11:11; Luke 7:28.

90. Cf. Matthew 6:24; Luke 16:13.

91. Cf. Mark 2:22; Matthew 9:17; Luke 5:37–39.

92. Cf. Mark 2:21; Matthew 9:16; Luke 5:36.

93. Cf. Gospel of Thomas 106; Mark 11:23; Matthew 17:20; 18:19; 21:21; Luke 17:6; 1 Corinthians 13:2.

94. Or, "solitary."

95. Cf. Gospel of Thomas 18.

96. Perhaps emend to read "<Who> are you?" (Coptic *entoten <nim>*).

97. This saying recalls the accounts of the career of the soul in a number of ancient texts, including gnostic texts, which describe the return of the soul to the exalted realm above—here understood to be the realm of light. In such accounts the powers of the cosmos often question the one passing through, and the soul is obliged to utter words of power in order to pass by the powers, be liberated from worldly existence, and return to the heavenly home. Cf. Mary Magdalene's vision of the soul in Gospel of Mary 15–17.

98. Here the Coptic text reads *anapausis*; Stephen Patterson, James M. Robinson, and Hans-Gebhard Bethge offer an emended text, to read "<resurrection>" (*ana<sta>sis*).

99. Cf. Luke 17:20–21; Gospel of Thomas 113; John 3:18–19; 5:25; 2 Timothy 2:17–18; Treatise on Resurrection 49.

100. Twenty-four is sometimes given as the number of books in the Jewish Scriptures.

101. Cf. Augustine of Hippo, *Contra adversarium legis et prophetarum* ("Against an Adversary of the Law and the Prophets") 2.4.14: "You have rejected the living one who is before you, and you speak idly of the dead." Perhaps also cf. Acts of Thomas 170.

102. Paul also refers to spiritual circumcision in Romans 2:25–29 and elsewhere.

103. Cf. Matthew 5:3; Luke 6:20.

104. This is a common figure of speech for bearing up under burdens or difficulties.

105. Cf. Mark 8:34; Matthew 10:37–38; 16:24; Luke 9:23; 14:26–27; Gospel of Thomas 101.

106. Cf. Gospel of Thomas 80. Here the saying reads "carcass" (*ptoma*); saying 80 reads "body" (*soma*).

107. Cf. Matthew 13:24–30.

108. Or, "Blessings on the person who has suffered."

109. Cf. Proverbs 8:34–36; Sirach 51:26–27; Gospel of Thomas 68–69.

110. Cf. Luke 17:22; John 7:33–36; 8:21; 13:33; Gospel of Thomas 38.

111. The emended reading (Coptic *<afnau>*) assumes letters similar to those at the end of saying 59 were omitted (haplography). Also possible is another, similar emendation, "<They saw>" (Coptic *<aunau>*).

112. Literally, "That person is around the lamb." The text may need to be emended to read, for example, "<Why does> that person <carry> around the lamb?" Patterson, Robinson, and Bethge accept a translation that assumes the Samaritan is trying to catch a lamb and is pursuing it.

113. Cf. Gospel of Thomas 7; 11.

114. The word translated "couch" (Coptic *cloc*) may also be translated "bed," but the saying probably refers to a couch used for dining.

115. Cf. Matthew 24:40–41; Luke 17:34–35.

116. Literally, "as from one." Layton, *Nag Hammadi Codex II*, 1.74, suggests two other options, both of which are based on possible mistranslations in the textual history of the Gospel of Thomas: "as from whom," from the Greek *hos ek tinos*, or "as a stranger," from the Greek *hos xenos*. Patterson, Robinson, and Bethge adopt the second of these options.

117. Cf. Matthew 11:27; Luke 10:22; John 3:35; 6:37–39; 13:3–4.

118. Here the Coptic is emended to read *efshe<sh>*, "<whole>"; the manuscript reads *efshef*, "desolate."

119. Cf. John 8:12.

120. Cf. Mark 4:11; Matthew 13:11; Luke 8:10. Hedrick, *Unlocking the Secrets of the Gospel according to Thomas*, 118, prefers to reconstruct this line to read "I tell my secrets to those who [seek my] secrets."

121. Cf. Matthew 6:3.

122. Cf. Luke 12:16–21; Sirach 11:18–19.

123. Cf. Matthew 22:1–14; Luke 14:16–24; Deuteronomy 20:5–7; 24:5.

124. Cf. Sirach 26:29.

125. This phrase may be restored to read "A usurer," "A creditor" (Coptic *ourome enkhre*[*ste*]*s*), as I prefer, or "A good person" (Coptic *ourome enkhre*[*sto*]*s*), with very different implications. In the first instance an abusive creditor may be understood as opposed by the victimized poor, in the second a good person may be interpreted as the victim of violent tenant farmers. I judge the former interpretation is more appropriate for the saying in Thomas and the teaching of Jesus.

126. This might be emended to read "Perhaps <they> did not know <him>."

127. Cf. Mark 12:1–9; Matthew 21:33–41; Luke 20:9–16.

128. Cf. Mark 12:10; Matthew 21:42; Luke 20:17; Acts 4:11; 1 Peter 2:7; Psalm 118:22.

129. Cf. Book of Thomas 138.

130. Cf. Matthew 5:10–11; Luke 6:22; Gospel of Thomas 58; 69. This saying could possibly be understood to mean that the place where they would not be persecuted might allude to the flight of early Christians from Jerusalem to Pella in Transjordan at the time of the first-century revolt against the Romans.

131. Cf. Gospel of Thomas 68.

132. Cf. Matthew 5:6; Luke 6:21. Hedrick, *Unlocking the Secrets of the Gospel according to Thomas*, 130, gives this translation of the second macarism: "'Those who go hungry to fill the starving belly of another are favored."

133. Cf. Gospel of Thomas 41; 67.

134. Cf. Mark 14:58; 15:29; Matthew 26:61; 27:40; John 2:19; Acts 6:14. The restoration "[again]" (Coptic *en*[*kesop*]) may presuppose a small blank space remaining at the end of the line. Patterson, Robinson, and Bethge accept the restoration "[except me]" (Coptic *en*[*sabellai*]).

135. Cf. Luke 12:13–14. 'Abd al-Jabbar, *Book on the Signs of Muhammad's Prophecy*, cites this saying: "A person said to him, 'Master, my brother (wants) to share (with me) my father's blessing.' (Jesus) said to him, 'Who placed me over you (to determine your) share?'"

136. Cf. Matthew 9:37–38; Luke 10:2; Mishnah, *Pirke Avot* 2.20.

137. Literally, "He said" (Coptic *pejaf*). Sayings 73–75 most likely should be read as a small dialogue. Cf. the Heavenly Dialogue in Origen, *Contra Celsum* (*Against Celsus*) 8.15: "If the son of God is stronger, and the child of humanity is his master—and who else will be master over the God who is mighty?—how is it that many are around the well and no one goes into the well? Why, when you have come to the end of so long a journey, are you lacking in daring?—You are mistaken, for I have courage and a sword."

138. Or, "no one" (Coptic *men laau*).

139. The word "<well>" (Coptic *sho<t>e*) is an emendation of the reading in the manuscript, "illness" (Coptic *shone*).

140. Or, "solitary."

141. Cf. Matthew 25:1–13.

142. Cf. Matthew 13:45–46.

143. Cf. Matthew 6:19–20; 13:44; Luke 12:33.

144. Cf. John 8:12; Wisdom of Solomon 7:24–30. Cf. also Manichaean Psalm Book 54,19–30: "The strangers with whom I mingled don't know me. They tasted my sweetness and wished to keep me with them. I became life for them, but they became death for me. I bore them up, and they wore me as a garment upon them. I am in all, I bear the heavens, I am the foundation, I support the earths, I am the light that shines forth, that makes the souls rejoice. I am the life of the world, I am the milk that is in all trees, I am the sweet water that is under the children of matter."

145. Cf. Romans 11:36; 1 Corinthians 8:6; Martyrdom of Peter 10.

146. Cf., perhaps, Lucian of Samosata, *Hermotimus* 81: "God is not in heaven but rather permeates all things, such as pieces of wood and stones and animals, even the most insignificant." The Greek Gospel of Thomas connects the last part of this saying with saying 30: "[Jesus says], 'Where there are [three, they are without] God, and where there is only [one], I say, I am with that one. Lift up the stone and you will find me there. Split the piece of wood, and I am there.'"

147. Cf. Matthew 11:7–8; Luke 7:24–25.

148. Cf. Luke 11:27–28.

149. Cf. John 13:17; James 1:25.

150. Cf. Mark 13:17; Matthew 24:19; Luke 21:23; 23:29. Also cf. the Gospel of the Egyptians: "Salome says reasonably, 'Until when will people die?' . . . Therefore the master answers in a circumspect manner, 'As long as women give birth.'"

151. Cf. Gospel of Thomas 56 and the note on *ptoma* and *soma*.

152. Cf. 1 Corinthians 4:8; Gospel of Thomas 110. Dialogue of the Savior 129, as reconstructed, cites a very similar saying of Jesus: "And I say to you, let one [who has] power renounce [it and] repent, and let one who [knows] seek and find and rejoice."

153. Very similar versions of this saying are known from a variety of sources, including Ignatius of Antioch, *To the Smyrnaeans* 4:2; nearly identical versions are cited in Origen, in Didymus the Blind, and in an Armenian text from the monastery of St. Lazzaro. The Gospel of the Savior reads, "If someone is near me, that person will [burn]. I am the fire that blazes. Whoever is [near me] is near the fire; whoever is far from me is far from life" (Berlin 2220 107,39–48; see Hedrick and Mirecki, *Gospel of the Savior*, 40–41). Greek proverbs also resemble saying 82: "Whoever is near Zeus is near the thunderbolt . . . far from Zeus and the thunderbolt."

154. Sayings 83–84 reflect themes in Genesis, especially Genesis 1:26–28, along with comments in Philo of Alexandria and gnostic texts on the creation

of humankind. Cf., for example, Philo, *Legum allegoriarum* (*Allegorical Inter-pretation of Genesis*) 1.31–32: "'And God formed humankind by taking clay from the earth, and he breathed into the face the breath of life, and humankind became a living soul.' There are two kinds of human beings: One is heavenly, the other earthly. Now the heavenly is made in the image of God and is completely free of corruptible and earthly substance; but the earthly was constructed from matter scattered about, which he (Moses) calls clay. Therefore he says that the heavenly human was not molded but was stamped in the image of God, while the earthly human is a molded thing, but not an offspring, of the Artisan. One must deduce that the human being from the earth is mind admitting but not yet penetrated by the body." The discussion of images in the Gospel of Thomas also recalls Platonic thought on the images and forms, and Platonic thought also influenced the Hellenistic Jewish author Philo of Alexandria.

155. Simon Magus claimed to be "the power of God that is called great" (cf. Acts 8:9–10), Yaldabaoth is said to have taken "great power" from his mother Wisdom in the Secret Book of John, and a Nag Hammadi tractate is titled Concept of Our Great Power.

156. Or, "son of man." This common phrase (here in Coptic *shere emprome*, from the Greek *huios tou anthropou*) often is translated "son of man" in other translations of Jewish and Christian texts. Sometimes it can mean a person, or it can be a way of referring to oneself in the first person singular, "I." Such seems to be the meaning here. At other times (as in the book of Daniel and other similar texts) it may have a more apocalyptic meaning.

157. Cf. Matthew 8:20; Luke 9:58; Plutarch, *Life of Tiberius Gracchus* 9.4–5. Also cf. al-Ghazali, *Revival of the Religious Sciences* 3.153: "It is recorded that one day Jesus was greatly troubled by the rain and thunder and lightning, and he began to seek shelter. His eye fell on a tent a ways away, but when he came to it, he found a woman inside, and so he turned away from it. Then he noticed a cave in a mountain, but when he came to it, there was a lion in it. Laying his hand on the lion, he said, 'My God, you've given everything a resting place, but to me have you given none.' Then God revealed to him, 'Your resting place is in the house of my mercy . . .'"

158. Cf. Gospel of Thomas 29; 112. Cf. also Pseudo-Macarius of Syria, *Homily* 1.11: "Shame on the body whenever it becomes fixed in its own nature, because it becomes corrupt and dies. And shame on the soul if it remains fixed only in its own nature and relies only upon its own works, not having commu-nion with the divine spirit, because it dies, not having been considered worthy of the eternal life of divinity."

159. Or, "angels."

160. Cf., perhaps, the owners of the world who reclaim garments in Gos-pel of Thomas 21, or those who receive the bodies of flesh from people in the Secret Book of John, or the dealers in bodies and souls in Authoritative Discourse. Or saying 88 may suggest interactions with teachers and prophets.

161. Cf. Matthew 23:25–26; Luke 11:39–41. Discussion in the Babylonian Talmud, *Berakoth* 51a and *Kelim* 25.1–9 offer similar insights.

162. Cf. Matthew 11:28–30; also the saying of Wisdom in Sirach 51:26–27: "Put your neck under the yoke, and let your soul receive instruction, it's nearby to find. See with your eyes that I have labored little and have found for myself much rest."

163. Cf. Matthew 16:1–3; Luke 12:54–56.

164. Cf. Gospel of Thomas 2; 94; Matthew 7:7–8; Luke 11:9–10.

165. Cf. John 16:4–5, 12–15, 22–28.

166. Cf. Matthew 7:6. The tentative restoration at the end of the saying (Coptic *shina je nouaaf enla[jte]*) seems appropriate in the context. Layton, *Nag Hammadi Codex II*, 1.86–87, suggests additional possible restorations: "They might bring it [to naught]"; "They might grind it [to bits]." Patterson, Robinson, and Bethge accept a restored reading close to the reading given here.

167. Cf. Gospel of Thomas 2; 92; Matthew 7:7–8; Luke 11:9–10.

168. Cf. Matthew 5:42; Luke 6:30, 34–35; Didache 1:5.

169. Cf. Matthew 13:33; Luke 13:20–21.

170. This parable is not attested elsewhere in early Christian literature, though Pseudo-Macarius of Syria tells a story about a bag of sand that leaks out through a tiny hole.

171. This parable is not attested elsewhere in early Christian literature—but cf., in general, Gospel of Thomas 35; Matthew 11:12–13; Luke 16:16.

172. Cf. Mark 3:31–35; Matthew 12:46–50; Luke 8:19–21; Gospel of the Ebionites 5.

173. Cf. Mark 12:13–17; Matthew 22:15–22; Luke 20:20–26.

174. The restoration adopted here is somewhat tentative (Coptic *entas[ti naei empc]ol*). Other possible readings include the following: "For my mother, who has [given birth to me, has destroyed me]." Cf. Layton, *Nag Hammadi Codex II*, 1.88; Patterson, Robinson, and Bethge leave the lacuna and add these two possible restorations in a note.

175. The true mother may be the holy Spirit. Cf. Gospel of the Hebrews 3; Secret Book of James 6; Gospel of Philip 55.

176. Cf. Matthew 10:37–38; Luke 12:26–27; Gospel of Thomas 55.

177. Cf. Matthew 23:13; Luke 11:52; Gospel of Thomas 39. Note may also be taken of Aesop, *Fable* 702: "A wicked dog was lying in a manger that was full of hay. When the cattle came to eat, it would not let them but bared its teeth in a threatening expression. The cattle then said to it, 'It is unfair for you to begrudge us the natural appetite that you do not have. For it is not your nature to eat hay, and yet you prevent us from eating it.'"

178. This phrase could refer either to the point in time or the point of location.

179. Cf. Gospel of Thomas 21; Matthew 24:43; Luke 12:39.

180. Cf. Mark 2:18–20; Matthew 9:14–15; Luke 5:33–35. The Gospel of the Nazoreans 2 reads as follows: "Look, the mother of the master and his brothers said to him 'John the baptizer is baptizing for the remission of sins. Let's go and be baptized by him.' But he said to them, 'What sin have I committed, that

I should hasten and be baptized by him? Unless perchance this very thing that I have said is ignorance.'"

181. The meaning of this saying remains obscure. It may suggest that one despise the physical connections of life (cf. Gospel of Thomas 55; 101; Book of Thomas 144). It may recall the figure of Helena, the prostitute from Tyre and the associate of Simon Magus who was actually the divine thought (cf. Irenaeus, *Against Heresies* 1.23.2). It may refer to the plight of the soul that falls into metaphorical prostitution (cf. the Nag Hammadi text Exegesis on the Soul). It may even point to the tradition that Jesus was the illegitimate child of Mary, who became pregnant, it sometimes is said, from a Roman soldier named Pantera or Panthera (cf. Origen, *Against Celsus* 1.28, 32; Talmudic sources and the Jewish text titled *Toledoth Yeshu*; perhaps John 8:41).

182. Cf. Gospel of Thomas 48; Mark 11:23; Matthew 17:20; 18:19; 21:21; Luke 17:6; 1 Corinthians 13:2.

183. Cf. Matthew 18:12–13; Luke 15:4–7; perhaps also Ezekiel 34:15–16.

184. Cf. Gospel of Thomas 13; John 4:13–14; 7:37–39; Sirach 24:21, on drinking of Wisdom.

185. Hedrick, *Unlocking the Secrets of the Gospel according to Thomas*, 180, restores this to read "[Before] he died" (Coptic *em[patfmou p]refmou*).

186. Cf. Proverbs 2:1–5; Sirach 20:30–31; Matthew 13:44. *Midrash Rabbah*, Song of Songs 4.12.1 has a similar story: "Rabbi Simeon ben Yohai taught, 'It is like a person who inherited some land that was a manure pile. Now the heir was lazy, and he went and sold it at a very low price. The buyer went to work and dug in it, and in it he found a treasure, and from that he built a great palace. The buyer began going around in public with servants following behind, from the treasure he got in it. Seeing this, the seller was ready to choke and said, 'Ah, what have I lost!'" So does Aesop, *Fable* 42: "A farmer who was about to die and who wished to familiarize his sons with farming summoned them and said, 'Sons, in one of my vineyards a treasure is hidden.' After his death they took plows and mattocks and dug up all of their farmed land. They did not find the treasure, but the vineyard repaid them with a harvest many times greater. The story shows that what is gotten from toil is a treasure for people."

187. Cf. Gospel of Thomas 27; 81.

188. A number of Jewish and early Christian texts describe the heavens being rolled up like a scroll. On living from the living one, cf. John 11:25–26.

189. This seems to be a later saying incorporated into the text.

190. Cf. Gospel of Thomas 29; 87.

191. Cf. Mark 13:21–23; Matthew 24:23–27; Luke 17:20–24; Gospel of Thomas 3. Especially cf. Gospel of Mary 8.

192. Although the language of this final saying in the Gospel of Thomas has become notorious for its apparent sexism—for good reason!—the saying apparently means to address gender categories in a more symbolic manner, typical of antiquity, with the female symbolizing what is earthly and perishable (like the earth Mother) and the male symbolizing what is heavenly and imperishable (like the sky Father). For the female to become male, then, all

that is mortal and a part of this world must become immortal and divine. The female becoming male and thus becoming complete also represents a particular ancient view of sexual difference, according to which a female is an incomplete male, without a penis, and she becomes complete when she is anatomically complete. Gospel of Thomas saying 22 is also concerned with images of human completeness, but it employs a different ancient view of sexual difference, according to which male and female come together as a single one, in androgynous union. Cf. Meyer, "Making Mary Male"; Meyer, "Gospel of Thomas Logion 114 Revisited." On Peter pitted against Mary and denouncing Mary, cf. Gospel of Mary 17–18; Pistis Sophia 36; 72; 146.

193. Knowledge.

194. Aeon.

3

MARY MAGDALENE

Although she is a woman in a book dominated by men, Mary Magdalene plays a substantial role as a figure in the entourage of Jesus
in the New Testament gospels.[1] In Luke 8:1–3 she is described in
the company of the Twelve, though not technically a part of the
inner circle of the Twelve. After a story of an unnamed woman,
a "sinner," who washes Jesus' feet with her tears, dries them with
her hair, and kisses and anoints them with myrrh (Luke 7:36–50),
Luke presents Mary Magdalene, or Mary of Magdala, in the company of other women:

> It happened soon afterward that Jesus was traveling
> through the towns and villages, preaching and announc-
> ing the good news of the kingdom of God. The Twelve
> were with him, as well as some women who had been
> cured of evil spirits and diseases: Mary, called Magda-
> lene, from whom seven demons had departed, and Joan-
> na, the wife of Chuza, Herod's steward, and Susanna, and
> many others who supported them with their resources.

Here Mary is said to have been cured of some psychological, men-
tal, or social issues by Jesus, and thereafter she helps in providing

1. For a fuller presentation and discussion of the ancient texts given here,
cf. Meyer, *The Gospels of Mary*.

support for Jesus and his disciples. Some have guessed that Mary may have been a woman of means, maybe a single woman, a divorced woman, or a widow. She came from Magdala, a city on the western shore of the Sea of Galilee that was well known for fishing and fish salting. As a woman, Mary Magdalene is significant in the New Testament gospel accounts, and in the lists of women that include Mary Magdalene, she nearly always is mentioned first—but she remains a woman, lingering on the periphery of the twelve disciples in the New Testament.

In the account of the crucifixion of Jesus in the New Testament, Mary and others are present at the cross, and after the death of Jesus she and her woman friends go to the tomb where Jesus was buried. In the Gospel of Mark, after all the male disciples have fled from the arrest and crucifixion of Jesus, Mary Magdalene and the other women encounter a youth (*neaniskos*) dressed in white and sitting inside Jesus' tomb—and then they, too, run away (16:1–8). In the Gospel of Matthew, Mary and her friend, another Mary, see an angel and not a youth, and then they meet Jesus himself, raised from the dead (28:1–10). In the Gospel of Luke, Mary and several other women see two men in dazzling garments—apparently also angels—and several appearances of the risen Christ are recorded (24:9–53). Mark 16:9–11, the longer (and somewhat later) ending of the Gospel of Mark, claims that Mary Magdalene is the first to have encountered the risen figure of Christ. So does the Gospel of John, with an intimate scene of Mary mistaking Jesus for the gardener, until Jesus calls her by her name: "Mary" (20:1–8). The closest parallel to this intimate scene in the Gospel of John seems to be in Song of Songs 3:1–5, where an account is given of a woman wandering about, seeking her lover, and finding him at last.[2]

The prominence of Mary Magdalene in the New Testament gospels provides hints of her importance in the Jesus movement. The New Testament is emphatic in depicting the Twelve as a specific group of twelve disciples, doubtless reflecting the twelve sons of Jacob and the twelve tribes of Israel as prototype of the church as a new Israel, and while the New Testament accounts are unanimous

2. Cf. Ruschmann, *Maria von Magdala im Johannesevangelium*, 201–7.

in identifying all the twelve disciples as males, the accounts differ on precisely what the names of some of the males might be. It seems very likely that the concept of the Twelve derives from the early church and is projected back upon the Jesus movement as described in the New Testament gospels. If that is the case, the suggestion of twelve guys in the inner circle of disciples around the historical Jesus may need to be abandoned, and the exclusion of Mary Magdalene from an inner circle of disciples may be reconsidered. Perhaps Mary Magdalene may be understood to be not merely a benefactress of Jesus but actually a disciple of Jesus, in every sense of the word. Further, as Esther de Boer has proposed,[3] there is evidence to support the theory that the beloved disciple in the Gospel of John could be none other than Mary Magdalene. The scene at the cross in John has Mary the mother of Jesus and the beloved disciple present there; Jesus says to his mother, "Woman, look, your son," and he says to the beloved disciple, "Look, your mother" (19:25–27). Traditionally the beloved disciple in this scene has been assumed to be John son of Zebedee, but no vocative is used in the words addressed to the beloved disciple so as to suggest that the beloved disciple was male. Could the beloved disciple be a woman—Mary Magdalene? De Boer writes,

> I conclude that Mary Magdalene should be seen as a serious candidate for the identification of the anonymous disciple Jesus loved in the Gospel of John. If we indeed look upon her as an important candidate, this has consequences for our general perspective on Mary Magdalene. She would have had disciples, her testimony would have formed a community, her accounts not only of the death and resurrection of Jesus, but also of his life and teachings, would have been preserved. But not only that, her words would have been canonized and taught through the ages, and spread over the world.[4]

---

3. De Boer, "Mary Magdalene and the Disciple Jesus Loved"; cf. Jusino, "Mary Magdalene: Author of the Fourth Gospel?"

4. De Boer, "Mary Magdalene and the Disciple Jesus Loved."

In other words, according to Esther de Boer, Mary Magdalene might even have been the author of the Gospel of John.

In the late sixth century, the image of Mary Magdalene was dealt a blow through the exegetical work and the subsequent preaching of Pope Gregory the Great. In *Homilia* (*Homily*) 33, delivered in the year 591 in Rome, Gregory the Great identifies Mary Magdalene with the woman who is called a sinner, that is, a prostitute, in Luke 7, thus connecting the accounts in Luke 7 and 8.[5] He declares, "We believe this woman—Mary Magdalene—is the female sinner in Luke, the woman John names Mary, the Mary from whom Mark states seven demons were cast out." Mary in the Gospel of John is the sister of Lazarus, who similarly is said to have anointed Jesus' feet with myrrh (12:1–8). The seven demons, Gregory the Great goes on to say, are seven vices, and elsewhere he discusses the seven deadly sins and connects them to these demons and vices. Here he maintains that the fragrant ointment the woman—now understood to be Mary Magdalene—used to anoint the feet of Jesus was what she also used to sweeten her skin for her lusty customers. The good news about Mary, he posits, is that she repented of her immoral life. The bad news is that after Gregory the Great, to the present, Mary Magdalene has been remembered in literature and art as the prostitute, the whore who repented of her wickedness, but still the repentant prostitute.

The biblical exegesis undertaken by Pope Gregory the Great is faulty. The women of Luke 7 and 8 should not be identified with each other, and in modern discussion scholars and theologians, including those who represent the Christian church, admit that Mary Magdalene should no longer be considered a prostitute. Nonetheless, the story of Mary as repentant prostitute makes for compelling literature, as we may see in *The Last Temptation of Christ* by Nikos Kazantzakis and other works. Museums around the world house images of Mary Magdalene, commonly depicted in voluptuous fashion as a woman with a sexual profession, now turning her life to the way of Jesus.

5. Cf. Haskins, *Mary Magdalen: The Essential History*; Schaberg, "How Mary Magdalene Became a Whore."

Meanwhile, since the discovery of the Gospel of Mary and related texts, the role of Mary Magdalene within the Jesus movement has been discussed with renewed enthusiasm by scholars and others. As the first to see the risen Christ, according to the Gospel of John and other texts, and the one charged with the task of communicating the gospel of the resurrection to the Twelve (or the Eleven, after the Judas Iscariot affair), she may be understood as the apostle to the apostles, but the Gospel of Mary portrays her place as even more central to the movement. In the Gospel of Mary, Mary Magdalene is the leading character, besides Jesus, in the account that unfolds. When the disciples are sad at the departure of Jesus, and begin to weep, it is Mary who comforts them. She is the one who proclaims the message of Jesus after he leaves, that Jesus has prepared the disciples and has made them truly human. Peter notes that Jesus loved Mary more than any of the other women, and he recognizes that there are things that Jesus told only to Mary, and so he asks her to share these matters with the other disciples. Mary does so, and she recounts a vision of the ascent of the soul (only partially preserved in the text). Near the conclusion of the gospel, Peter and Andrew raise serious doubts about whether Jesus said all these things to a woman, in private. But Levi silences Peter by calling to mind his infamous temper, and he reminds Peter and the others that Jesus loved Mary most, more than the other disciples.

In the Gospel of Mary, Mary Magdalene clearly may be taken to be a disciple of Jesus, and she is portrayed as a beloved disciple. The conflict with Peter, though less reflective of any historical conflict between the two individuals than indicative of disagreements and rivalries in the early church, highlights the position of Mary as an authoritative figure in the Jesus movement. Karen King explains it like this in *The Gospel of Mary: Jesus and the First Woman Apostle*:

> The portrait of Mary Magdalene in the Gospel of Mary offers an alternative to sole reliance on apostolic witness as the source of authority. Although she, too, knew the historical Jesus, was a witness to the resurrection,

and received instruction from the savior, these experiences are not what set her apart from the others. Mary is clearly portrayed throughout the gospel as an exemplary disciple. She does not falter when the savior departs. She steps into his place after his departure, comforting, strengthening, and instructing the others. Her spiritual comprehension and spiritual maturity are demonstrated in her calm behavior and especially in her visionary experience. These at once provide evidence of her spiritual maturity and form the basis for her legitimate exercise of authority in instructing the other disciples. She does not teach in her own name but passes on the words of the savior, calming the disciples, and turning their hearts toward the good. Her character proves the truth of her teaching, and by extension authorizes the teaching of the Gospel of Mary—and it does so by opposing her to those apostles who reject women's authority and preach another gospel, laying down laws beyond that which the savior taught.[6]

Elsewhere in early Christian literature, particularly in gnostic texts, Mary Magdalene is also singled out for her role as disciple, and sometimes beloved disciple. (Another woman, Salome, also calls herself a disciple of Jesus in Gospel of Thomas 61.) Mary is not the only disciple termed beloved, of course. There are almost too many beloved disciples in early Christian literature, and there may be competition in the early church about which disciple Jesus loved most. We might imagine that a given community could champion their favorite disciple as the one Jesus loved most— "Jesus loved our disciple more than yours."[7] The candidates for beloved disciple include (in no particular order): the youth (*neaniskos*) in the Gospel of Mark and Secret Mark; Lazarus in the Gospel of John; perhaps John son of Zebedee; Judas Thomas the Twin; James the Just, the brother of Jesus, in the Secret Book of James and the First Revelation of James; Peter, also in the Secret Book of James; and even—with a bit of a stretch—Judas Iscariot in the

6. King, *The Gospel of Mary*, 73–74.

7. Cf. Meyer, "Whom Did Jesus Love Most? Beloved Disciples in John and Other Gospels."

Gospel of Judas. In the Gospel of Philip from the Nag Hammadi library (Codex II,3), Mary Magdalene is called the companion or partner of Jesus (*koinonos*, from Greek, and *hotre*, in Coptic), and it is stated that Jesus loved Mary Magdalene more than the other disciples and kissed her often—but precisely where he kissed her is lost in a lacuna. (Many scholars restore the text to read "on her [mouth]," but other possible body parts remain.) The message of the Gospel of Philip does not necessarily mean that there was a physical or sexual relationship between Jesus and Mary (nor does the wording of the text completely exclude such a possibility). The emphasis in the Gospel of Philip, as in the Gospel of Mary, is on the spiritual connection between Jesus and Mary.

In the Dialogue of the Savior, also from the Nag Hammadi library (Codex III,5), Mary Magdalene is in close conversation with Jesus, along with Matthew and Judas, and she herself utters words of wisdom reminiscent of sayings of Jesus:

> The wickedness of each day <is sufficient>.
> Workers deserve their food.
> Disciples resemble their teachers. (139)

For these observations she is praised as "a woman who understood everything (or, completely, *epteref*)." In the Pistis Sophia, as in the Gospel of Thomas and the Gospel of Mary, Mary Magdalene is opposed by Peter, but in the Pistis Sophia she is arguably the most engaged of the disciples, and she offers interpretations of sayings of Jesus and scriptural passages. Jesus says to Mary, "You are one whose heart is set on the kingdom of heaven more than all your brothers" (17), and he tells her, "You are more blessed than all women on earth" (19). Mary is, according to Jesus in the Pistis Sophia, "pure spiritual woman" (87).[8] The Manichaean Psalms of Heracleides call Mary "the spirit of wisdom" (194), and extol her for her ministry on behalf of Jesus:

> Glory to Mary,
> because she has listened to her master,
> [she has] carried out his instructions
> with joy in her whole heart. (187)

8. Coptic *tepneumatike enhilikrines*.

Jane Schaberg summarizes the historical data well in her popular article about Mary Magdalene: "Mary Magdalene is in fact the primary witness to the fundamental data of early Christian faith."[9] Once considered, wrongly, to be a whore, Mary is now seen to be a close disciple, a beloved disciple, of Jesus. Fresh insights into New Testament texts and the discovery of new texts reveal Mary Magdalene as nothing less than a founding mother of early Christianity.

❧

The Gospel of Mary is available in Coptic as the opening tractate of the Berlin Gnostic Codex (Papyrus Berolinensis) 8502. Two Greek fragments, Papyrus Oxyrhynchus 3525 and Papyrus Rylands 463, have also been recovered. The Coptic text is translated below, and significant variants in the Greek fragments are mentioned in the notes. The Coptic text of the Gospel of Mary is most well preserved, but even so it is missing six manuscript pages at the beginning and four manuscript pages in the middle of the text. The middle portion of the text, with an account of Mary's vision of the ascent of the soul, may be more fully understood and interpreted on the basis of fragments placed in the fourth text of Codex Tchacos, provisionally titled Book of Allogenes. Archeological work continues at the site of Magdala, modern-day Migdal, on the shores of the Sea of Galilee. The Gospel of Mary was most likely composed in Greek, in Syria or Egypt, in the second century. Like the Gospel of Thomas, the Gospel of Mary may not be classified as a gnostic text without considerable qualification. Some prefer to call it—like the Thomas Gospel—a gnosticizing text, a text bearing some resemblance to gnostic texts and sharing the pages of a codex with gnostic texts. Greco-Roman philosophical influences in the Gospel of Mary, especially Platonic and Stoic influences, may be more apparent.

9. Schaberg, "How Mary Magdalene Became a Whore."

༺ঽ

Additional reading: Bernabé Ubieta, *Maria Magdalena: Tradiciones en el Cristianismo Primitivo*; Brock, *Mary Magdalene, the First Apostle*; de Boer, *The Gospel of Mary: Beyond a Gnostic and a Biblical Mary Magdalene*; de Boer, *Mary Magdalene: Beyond the Myth*; Haskins, *Mary Magdalen: The Essential History*; Haskins, *Mary Magdalen: Myth and Metaphor*; Hearon, *The Mary Magdalene Tradition: Witness and Counter-Witness*; Jones, *Which Mary? The Marys of Early Christian Tradition*; Jusino, "Mary Magdalene: Author of the Fourth Gospel?"; King, *The Gospel of Mary: Jesus and the First Woman Apostle*; Marjanen, *The Woman Jesus Loved: Mary Magdalene in the Nag Hammadi Library and Related Documents*; Meyer, *The Gospels of Mary*; Pasquier, *L'Évangile selon Marie*; Ruschmann, *Maria von Magdala im Johannesevangelium*; Schaberg, "How Mary Magdalene Became a Whore"; Schaberg, *The Resurrection of Mary Magdalene*; Scopello, *Femme, gnose et manichéisme*; Torjesen, *When Women Were Priests*.

Translation: The Gospel of Mary

After a Long Break at the Opening of the Text, the Disciples Are in Dialogue with the Savior about the Nature of Matter[1]

". . . Will matter be destroyed, or not?"[2]

The savior replied, "All natures, all things formed, all creatures exist in and with one another, and they will dissolve into their own root. For the nature of matter is dissolved into what is at the root of its nature.[3]

"If you have ears to hear, you should hear."

Peter said to him, "You have told us everything. Explain to us this also: what is the sin of the world?"

The savior answered, "There is no such thing as sin. You create sin when you commingle as in adultery, and that is what is called sin. That is why the good came among you, to those of each nature, to restore each nature to its root."[4]

He went on: "For this reason you get sick and die, for [you love] [8] what [deceives you].

"If you have a mind, you should understand.

"Matter gave birth to passion that is without form, since it comes from what is contrary to nature, and then confusion arose in the entire body. For this reason I told you, Be of good courage.[5] And should you be discouraged, be of courage in the presence of nature's diversity of forms.[6]

"If you have ears to hear, you should hear."

After the blessed one said this, he welcomed all of them and said, "Peace be with you; receive my peace.[7] Take care that no one deceives you by saying, 'Look, here,' or 'Look, there.'[8] The child of humanity[9] is within you.[10] Follow that.[11] Those who seek it will find it.[12] Go out and preach the message of good news about the kingdom. Do not [9] make any rules other than what I have given you, and do not lay down law, as the lawgiver has done, or you will be bound by it."

Having said this, he left them.[13]

Mary Comforts the Disciples and Recalls
a Conversation with the Master

The disciples were upset and wept profoundly, and they said, "How can we go to the gentile world and preach the message of good news about the kingdom of the child of humanity? If they didn't spare him, how will they spare us?"[14]

Mary stood up and gave greetings to them all.[15] She said to her brothers, "Do not weep or be upset or in doubt, for his grace will abide with you all and protect you. Rather, we should praise his greatness, for he has prepared us and made us human."

When Mary said this, she moved their hearts toward the good, and they began to discuss the [savior's] words. [**10**]

Peter said to Mary, "Sister, we know the savior loved you more than all other women.[16] Tell us the savior's words as you remember them, words you know but we don't, since we haven't heard them."

Mary replied and said, "What is hidden from you I shall teach you."

And she began to speak these words to them.

She said, "I saw the master[17] in a vision, and I said to him, 'Master, I saw you in a vision today.'

"He replied and said to me, 'Blessings on you, since you did not waver when you saw me. For where the mind is the treasure is.'[18]

"I asked him, 'Master, how does a person behold a vision? With soul or spirit?'

'The savior answered and said, 'A person beholds with neither soul nor spirit. The mind, which is between the two, beholds the vision . . .'"[19]

After Another Break in the Text, Mary Is Recounting Her
Vision of the Ascent of the Soul[20]

"Desire said, 'I did not see you going down, but now I see you rising. Why are you lying, since you belong to me?'

"The soul answered and said, 'I saw you but you did not see me or know me. To you I was merely a garment,[21] and you did not recognize me.'

"After the soul said this, she left, with great joy.

"The soul came to the third power, named ignorance. The power interrogated the soul, saying, 'Where are you going? You are bound by wickedness, you are bound. Do not judge.'

"The soul said, 'Why do you judge me, though I have not judged? I have been bound, but I have not bound. I was not recognized, but I have recognized that all is to be dissolved, both the earthly [16] and the heavenly.'

"When the soul subdued the third power, she rose and saw the fourth power. It took seven forms:

The first form is darkness.
The second is desire.
The third is ignorance.
The fourth is death wish.
The fifth is kingdom of flesh.
The sixth is foolish wisdom of flesh.
The seventh is hothead's wisdom.

These are the seven powers of wrath.[22]

"The powers asked the soul, 'Where are you coming from, slayer of humans, and where are you going, destroyer of worlds?'

"The soul answered and said, 'What binds me is slain and what surrounds me is destroyed. My desire is gone. Ignorance is dead. In a world I was freed [17] through[23] another world, and in an image I was freed through a heavenly image. The fetter of forgetfulness is passing. From this moment on I shall rest, through the time of the age, in silence.'"

After Mary said this, she stopped talking, because the savior had said this much to her.

Peter and Andrew Express Doubts about Mary's Words

Andrew replied and said to the brothers, "Say what you will about what she has told us, but I don't believe the savior said these things. These teachings are very strange."

Peter expressed similar concerns. He questioned the others about the savior: "Did he really speak with a woman in private without our knowledge? Should we all turn and listen to her? Did he favor her over us?"²⁴ [**18**]

Levi Expresses Support for Mary, and the Disciples Depart to Teach and Preach

Then Mary wept and said to Peter, "My brother Peter, what are you thinking? Do you think I made all this up myself, and that I am telling lies about the savior?"

Levi answered and said to Peter, "Peter, you are always a hothead. Now I see you arguing against this woman like the adversaries. If the savior made her worthy, who are you to turn her away? Certainly the savior knows her very well. That's why he loved her more than us.²⁵

"So, we should be ashamed, and put on perfect humanity and acquire it, as he commanded us, and preach the good news, and not make any rule or law other than what the savior stated."

After [**19**] [he said] this, they got up and went out [to] teach and preach.²⁶

The Gospel according to Mary

Endnotes

1. Berlin Gnostic Codex 8502,1: 7,1—19,5. For the Berlin Gnostic Codex Coptic text and the Greek fragments, cf. Parrott, *Nag Hammadi Codices V,2–5 and VI with Papyrus Berolinensis 8502,1 and 4*; Till and Schenke, *Die gnostischen Schriften des koptischen Papyrus Berolinensis 8502*; Lührmann, "Die griechischen Fragmente des Mariaevangeliums POxy 3525 und PRyl 463." For translations of and commentaries on the Gospel of Mary, cf. de Boer, *The Gospel of Mary: Beyond a Gnostic and a Biblical Mary Magdalene*; King, *The Gospel of Mary: Jesus and the First Woman Apostle*; Pasquier, *L'Évangile selon Marie*. Pages 1–6 are missing from the Coptic manuscript.

2. As the text of the extant manuscript begins on page 7, Jesus and the disciples are engaged in a conversation, typical of philosophical schools, about whether matter is preexistent and eternal, or created and destined for dissolution.

3. On the nature of matter, compare, with Karen King (*The Gospel of Mary of Magdala: Jesus and the First Woman Apostle*, 45), the report by Cicero,

Academica Posteriora (*Academics* 1) 1.27, about the position of the Platonists: "they hold that underlying all things is a substance called 'matter', entirely formless and devoid of all 'quality', . . . and that out of it all things have been formed and produced, so that this matter can in its totality receive all things and undergo every sort of transformation throughout every part of it, and in fact even suffers dissolution, not into nothingness but into its own parts." Note may also be taken of Gospel of Philip 53: "Light and darkness, life and death, and right and left are siblings of one another, and inseparable. For this reason the good are not good, the bad are not bad, life is not life, death is not death. Each will dissolve into its original nature, but what is superior to the world cannot be dissolved, for it is eternal."

4. Improper commingling, comparable to metaphysical adultery, involves the mixing of the spiritual and the material. As the words of Jesus in the text maintain, such commingling leads to nothing but grief. Still, the coming of the good, apparently God, can restore a person's connection with his or her spiritual root, or spiritual nature. Cf. Gospel of Philip 61, with reference to the Genesis story: "And what nobility this is! First came adultery, then murder. One was born of adultery, for he was the son of the serpent. He became a murderer, like his father, and he killed his brother. Every act of sexual intercourse between those unlike each other is adultery." Cf. also Paul's discussion of sin in Romans 7.

5. Cf. Luke 24:38; John 14:27.

6. On sickness and passion, compare, with Esther de Boer (*The Gospel of Mary: Beyond a Gnostic and a Biblical Mary Magdalene*, 42), the Stoic position reported by Stobaeus, *Anthologium* (*Anthology*) 2.93.1–13: "Proneness to sickness is a tendency toward passion, toward one of the functions contrary to nature, such as depression, irascibility, malevolence, quick temper, and the like. Proneness to sickness also occurs in reference to other functions which are contrary to nature, such as theft, adultery, and violence; hence people are called thieves, violators, and adulterers. Sickness is an appetitive opinion which has flowed into a tenor and hardened, signifying a belief that what should not be pursued is intensely worth pursuing, such as the passion for women, wine, and money. By antipathy the opposites of the sicknesses occur, such as loathing for women and wine, and misanthropy." In this section Karen King prefers to translate "form" (Coptic *eine*) as "image," and suggests that the true images of nature are those that derive from God.

7. Cf. John 14:27; 20:19, 21, 26.

8. Cf. Gospel of Thomas 113.

9. Or, "son of man," here and below.

10. Cf. Luke 17:21; Gospel of Thomas 3.

11. Or, "him," here and below.

12. On this passage cf. Gospel of Thomas 108.

13. This is a reference either to the crucifixion or the resurrection and ascension of Jesus. I favor the interpretation of the departure as the crucifixion and death of Jesus.

14. Jesus was not spared in that he was crucified.

15. Papyrus Oxyrhynchus 3525 adds that Mary also kissed them tenderly.

16. That Mary is loved by Jesus is also maintained by other texts, especially the Gospel of Philip 59; 63–64; and Pistis Sophia 17; 19; cf. also Gospel of Mary 17–18. Jesus says to Mary, in Pistis Sophia 19, "You are more blessed than all women on earth, because you will be the fullness of fullnesses and the completion of completions."

17. Or, "lord," here and below.

18. Cf. Matthew 6:21.

19. Jesus in the Gospel of Mary is said to affirm that such a vision is not a purely emotional experience of the soul, nor is it a purely spiritual inspiration from outside oneself. Rather, a true vision entails insight of the mind. One thinks a vision. At this point in the papyrus the text breaks off and disappears into a long lacuna; the last words of text remaining before the lacuna are "and that is [what] . . . ."

20. Pages 11–14 are missing from the manuscript. The text resumes as Mary is discussing the vision she experienced of the ascent of the soul. Here feminine pronouns are used in reference to the soul, because in Greek the word for "soul," *psukhe*, is feminine in gender. The soul commonly is personified in Greek mythology as the young woman Psyche, who is associated with the figure of Eros (or, Cupid), "Love." The vision recounted in the Gospel of Mary depicts the soul ascending past four powers, perhaps thought to be the four elements of this world. It may be speculated that the name of the first power, lost in the lacuna, could be "darkness," on the basis of the list of the seven forms of the fourth, composite power. The list of the four powers and the seven forms of the fourth power may suggest that a scribe secondarily assembled two lists into one. Now, with the placement of new fragments in the fourth text of Codex Tchacos, the so-called Book of Allogenes, an account of the ascent of Allogenes the Stranger, who is Jesus, provides a description of Allogenes being freed from the grasp of several authorities (probably seven in number) on his way upward, to his Father, and this passage closely parallels the vision in the Gospel of Mary. In the Book of Allogenes, Allogenes is told that he will fall into the hands of several authorities, but that he will be liberated from their power. To each authority he says, with minor variations, "What binds me is slain, and I have been released, and I shall go up to my Father, who is above all these great aeons." The seven authorities are named, in the Book of Allogenes, desire, darkness, ignorance, death wish, kingdom of flesh, foolish fleshly wisdom, and (perhaps, we might guess, though the name is in a lacuna) hothead's wisdom. Each time Allogenes utters the statement of release, the text promises, he will be released from the power of the authority. See Wurst, "Weitere neue Fragmente aus Codex Tchacos." (The placement of these new fragments in the Book of Allogenes is based on work undertaken by Hans-Gebhard Bethge, Marvin Meyer, Uwe-Karsten Plisch, and Gregor Wurst at a seminar in Augsburg, Germany, during June–July 2011.) On what is bound being slain and the promise of release, compare Gospel of Mary 16–17.

Accounts of the soul ascending through the realms of the powers, being inter-rogated, and finally being set free are to be found in a number of texts relating to gnostic and gnosticizing spirituality (for example, the First Revelation of James from the Nag Hammadi library, also known as the tractate James from Codex Tchacos). Cf. also Gospel of Thomas 50.

21. In ancient Greco-Roman thought, the body and all those features that characterize bodily existence could be called a garment clothing the soul. Ac-cordingly, the soul may be described putting on the garment when it enters the world and taking it off when it leaves the world.

22. On seven cosmic powers, perhaps compare the heavenly spheres (com-monly for the sun, moon, and five planets—Mercury, Venus, Mars, Jupiter, Saturn) referred to by ancient astronomers and astrologers.

23. Or, "from," here and later in the sentence.

24. On the hostility of Peter toward Mary, cf. Gospel of Thomas 114; Pis-tis Sophia 36; 72; 146. According to Pistis Sophia 36, Peter complains about Mary to Jesus, "My master, we can't endure this woman who gets in our way and doesn't let any of us speak, though she talks all the time," and Mary later responds to Jesus, in Pistis Sophia 72, "I'm afraid of Peter, because he threatens me and hates our gender."

25. On the love of Jesus for Mary, cf. Gospel of Mary 10; Gospel of Philip 59; 63–64; Pistis Sophia 17; 19. According to Gospel of Philip 63–64, "The companion of the [savior] is Mary Magdalene. The [savior loved] her more than [all] the disciples, [and he] kissed her often on her [mouth (?)]. The other [disciples] . . . said to him, 'Why do you love her more than all of us?' The savior answered and said to them, 'Why don't I love you like her? If a blind person and one who can see are both in darkness, they are the same. When the light comes, one who can see will see the light, and the blind person will stay in darkness.'" See also the discussion on the beloved disciple in the introduction to this chapter.

26. Papyrus Rylands 463 states that it was Levi who left in order to preach.

4

JUDAS ISCARIOT

One of the most intriguing figures in all of early Christian literature is Judas Iscariot, the disciple of Jesus who is described turning
his friend over to the Roman authorities to be crucified.[1] While
Paul seems to know nothing of Judas, the Gospel of Mark singles
out Judas as the disciple who hands Jesus over, though he does not
clarify the motive for or the precise nature of the act (14:10–50).
Mark employs the Greek verb *paradidonai* to describe Jesus being
handed over or betrayed (as translations usually word it). Paul uses
the same verb to indicate that Jesus was handed over to be execut-
ed, but Paul states that it was God who handed Jesus over (Romans
8:31–32), or Jesus handed himself over (Galatians 2:19–20). The
Gospel of Matthew builds upon Mark's account, and explains that
Judas betrayed Jesus for money and felt so regretful afterwards that
he went out and killed himself by hanging (26:14—27:10). Luke
intensifies the heinous character of the act by insisting that the
devil made Judas do what he did (22:3), and in the Acts of the
Apostles, Judas is said to have taken a horrific fall, so that his belly
burst open and he died (1:13–26). In the Gospel of John, Judas is
identified as a devil (6:70), "the son of perdition" (17:12). Thus,
during the last decades of the first century, the accounts of the
handing over and crucifixion of Jesus in the New Testament show
an escalation of hostility toward Judas and his role.

1. For a fuller presentation and discussion of the ancient and late antique
texts given here, cf. Ehrman, *The Lost Gospel of Judas Iscariot*; Meyer, *Judas*.

The vilification of Judas Iscariot continues in the second century and beyond. According to the Arabic Infancy Gospel, young Judas spent time in the neighborhood where Jesus lived, and a demon came upon him. Judas goes after Jesus and tries to bite him, but he cannot, so he hits Jesus on his side. In the *Expositiones oraculorum dominicorum* (*Expositions of the Sayings of the Lord*), Papias presents Judas as a repulsive, obese figure: "He grew to be so bloated in his flesh that he could not squeeze through an opening a chariot could easily go through—not even his bulging head" (book 4, frag. 4). Judas is altogether disgusting, and even his putrid corpse leaves a horrible stench where he died. In the Paschal Hymn of Sedulius, the author attempts to fashion an epic poem about Jesus after the order of the Roman poet Virgil, and in the lines about Judas he piles term upon term as he expresses his animosity toward the traitor. A tale in a text often referred to as the Gospel of Bartholomew portrays Mrs. Judas as an unscrupulous woman with insatiable greed, who drives her husband to betray Jesus for money. She works as a wet nurse, and the baby boy of Joseph of Arimathea refuses to take milk from her wicked breast. Another text, known under the title of the Gospel of Nicodemus, has Judas go to his wife, in despair, with the intention of hanging himself, because, he says, he has betrayed Jesus, and when Jesus rises from the dead, he will be furious. The wife of Judas assures her husband, "Don't speak or think like that. For it is just as possible for this cock roasting over the charcoal fire to crow as for Jesus to rise again, as you are saying." The cock does crow—and Judas goes out and hangs himself.

The tall tales go on. According to the Acts of Andrew and Paul, Judas repents of his actions, and reminds Jesus of the need to forgive seventy times seven times, but he ends up worshiping the devil after all. In the Gospel of Barnabas, composed under Islamic influence, Judas is mistaken for Jesus, and he is crucified, not Jesus. The Golden Legend narrates a story of Judas that parallels the story of Oedipus from Greek mythology: Judas kills his father Ruben and marries his mother Ciborea, and then he sells his master Jesus for thirty coins. In Dante's *Inferno* Judas is confined in the lowest circle of hell, with Brutus and Cassius, who, as assassins of Julius Caesar, are guilty of the same sort of reprehensible deed as Judas.

Yet, through all these imaginative stories, most of which paint a picture of a demonized Judas, Judas Iscariot continues to attract our attention for the ambiguities of his complex character, and hints of a more positive Judas may be recognized from the earliest accounts.[2] As noted, Paul never mentions a betrayal of Jesus by Judas Iscariot, and he understands Jesus being handed over to death in a very different, upbeat light. Where he is mentioned, Judas is usually named Judas Iscariot. The meaning of Iscariot has been debated, but most likely it means "man of Kerioth," a southern town in Judea.[3] If this is the correct meaning, Judas could be a man not of Galilee but of the south, the region around Jerusalem. A popular theory, though less likely, proposes that "Iscariot" derives from the Latin *sicarius* (plural, *sicarii*) and makes him a dagger man—the *sicarii* was a group of first-century assassins who targeted Jerusalem elites they considered Roman collaborators. This theory would maintain that Judas may have been a Jewish[4] patriot with a strongly anti-Roman political vision of the kingdom of God, and he may have brought this vision to the circle of disciples around Jesus. Additionally, in the New Testament gospel accounts, Judas is in the inner circle of the disciples, one of the Twelve, and he is the keeper of the finances for the group and is present with the others at the last supper.

In the conversation at the last supper, according to the Gospel of John (13:27), Jesus tells Judas to do what he must do, and do it quickly, as if Jesus is fully aware of, and perhaps complicitous with, the plans of Judas. This possible interpretation leads William Klassen to focus attention, in his book *Judas: Betrayer or Friend of Jesus?*, on the more benign meaning of *paradidonai* as "hand over." He proposes that Judas merely intended to arrange a meeting

---

2. Cf. Klassen, *Judas: Betrayer or Friend of Jesus?*; Meyer, *The Gospel of Judas: On a Night with Judas Iscariot*; Paffenroth, *Judas: Images of the Lost Disciple*.

3. For other meanings of the term Iscariot, cf. Meyer, *Judas*, 150–51 n. 29.

4. Or, perhaps more accurately, "Judean," here and below.

between Jesus and the Jewish authorities, and something went terribly wrong. Klassen writes,

> What precisely was Judas's contribution? I submit that in the grand scheme of things, it was quite modest. In discussions with Jesus, he had often heard Jesus criticize the Temple hierarchy. When Judas reminded Jesus that his own advice had always been to rebuke the sinner directly, Jesus may have said that an occasion to confront the high priest directly had not appeared. Perhaps at that point Judas offered to arrange it, hoping that the process of rebuke would work. At the same time, he may have questioned Jesus about his own faithfulness to his mission. All of this could have led to a plan whereby Judas would arrange a meeting with Jesus and the high priest, each agreeing to that meeting on their own terms and with their own hopes for the outcome. This role in the "handing over" was later transformed into a more sinister one, especially after Judas died at his own hand. Whether the reader is able to accept this interpretation of the earliest traditions available to us, I submit that it is at least as plausible as the very negative view of Judas that still pervades the church but rests on a very shaky foundation.[5]

The discovery of the Gospel of Judas has reinvigorated the discussion of Judas Iscariot and Judas traditions. Unlike the Gospels of Thomas and Mary, which cannot be referred to as gnostic without qualification, the Gospel of Judas can be called, unequivocally, a gnostic gospel.[6] The Gospel of Judas reflects what most scholars describe as Sethian thought.[7] Sethians are assigned this

5. Klassen, *Judas: Betrayer or Friend of Jesus?*, 74.

6. On the use of the word "gnostic," cf. Brakke, *The Gnostics*; King, *What Is Gnosticism?*; Marjanen, *Was There a Gnostic Religion?*; Meyer, *The Gnostic Discoveries*, 38–43; Williams, *Rethinking "Gnosticism"*.

7. Cf. Meyer, "Judas and the Gnostic Connection," in Kasser, Meyer, and Wurst, *The Gospel of Judas* (2nd ed.), 125–54; Meyer, "When the Sethians Were Young"; Schenke, "The Phenomenon and Significance of Sethian Gnosticism"; Schenke, "Das sethianische System nach Nag-Hammadi-Handschriften"; Turner, "Sethian Gnosticism: A Literary History"; Turner, *Sethian Gnosticism and the Platonic Tradition*; Williams, "Sethianism."

name on account of their allegiance to the tradition of Seth, the good son of Adam and Eve who is born after the unfortunate events that transpired in the first, dysfunctional family according to the book of Genesis. Irenaeus of Lyon writes in his tract *Against Heresies* (*Adversus haereses*) that such people of Seth call themselves "gnostics," people of knowledge and insight (*gnosis*); for this reason Bentley Layton recognizes them as "classic gnostics."[8] Among the gnostic texts discussed by Irenaeus, and even referred to by name, is the Gospel of Judas, and the précis of the Gospel of Judas in Irenaeus (*Against Heresies* 1.31.1) compares well with the contents of the actual Gospel of Judas.[9] In the Gospel of Judas, the human protagonist is Judas Iscariot. Among the disciples, only he has the strength and courage to stand before Jesus, and only he has the correct profession, from a Sethian gnostic point of view, of who Jesus is (35). Throughout the text Judas is in dialogue with Jesus, and Judas is singled out to receive much of the wisdom and knowledge Jesus has to communicate.

As in the broader Judas tradition, all the news about Judas in the Gospel of Judas is not uniformly good, and he is described as a "spirit" or "demon" (*daimon*, 44), whose star is destined for "the thirteenth aeon" (55), a heavenly locale thought to be beyond the world below and the twelve signs of the zodiac and on the border of the infinite, in a place with a degree of cosmological ambivalence.[10] That the description of Judas in the Gospel of Judas would suggest that he is opposed and ostracized fits the style of gnostic texts, which see a heroic quality in figures who are in disfavor with the powers of this world, including the demiurge, the creator of this world. Judas's place in the Gospel of Judas recalls the figure of Sophia, personified Wisdom, who frequently appears in gnostic texts and who is also described, in the Pistis Sophia, the Books of Jeu, and elsewhere, as a "spirit" or "demon" bound for "the

8. Layton, *The Gnostic Scriptures.*

9. Cf. Wurst, "Irenaeus of Lyon and the Gospel of Judas," in Kasser, Meyer, and Wurst, *The Gospel of Judas* (2nd ed.), 169–79.

10. For more on the themes in this paragraph, see the notes to the translation.

thirteenth aeon." Irenaeus even observes that some folks, probably followers of the teacher Valentinus, compared the figures of Judas and Sophia (*Against Heresies* 2.20). The experiences of both Judas and Wisdom illustrate the life of the soul of the gnostic in this world, opposed by the megalomaniacal forces of the world, but endowed with knowledge, enlightened with insight, and looking to achieve peace and rest.

At the conclusion of the Gospel of Judas, Judas hands Jesus—or rather, the mortal body of Jesus—over to the authorities, and although the spiritual person of Jesus has been liberated from the body and the sting of the betrayal is absent from the account, the scene still raises the issue of the position of the betrayal story in the narrative of the passion of Jesus in early Christian literature. Throughout the New Testament gospels the story of Jesus is formed with references to passages from the Jewish Scriptures, and in a manner that recalls aspects of Jewish midrash and the pesharim from among the Dead Sea Scrolls, scenes in the life of Jesus are created with elements from these scriptural passages. To this extent, a goodly amount of the story of Jesus may be considered fiction, pious fiction, created on the basis of themes lifted from the holy scriptures. Such may also be the case with the story of Judas Iscariot, and parallels in the Jewish Scriptures to moments in the story of Judas would seem to confirm this.[11] Before Judas, Joab prepared to kiss Amasa and then killed him (2 Samuel 20); thirty pieces of silver was the price for a slave (Exodus 21) or for the shepherd king (Zechariah 11); and duplicitous people like Korah, Dathan, Abiram, Absalom, and Amasa died badly. Ahithophel turned against King David, and when his counsel was rejected by Absalom, he went out and hanged himself (2 Samuel 15–17). Before Judas, in a variety of texts of world literature, including Jewish texts, stories of betrayal were told, gripping tales of friend turning

11. Cf. Maccoby, *Judas Iscariot and the Myth of Jewish Evil*; Meyer, *The Gospel of Judas: On a Night with Judas Iscariot*; Meyer, "Jesus, Judas Iscariot, and the *Gospel of Judas*"; Spong, *Liberating the Gospels: Reading the Bible with Jewish Eyes*.

against friend and brother against brother.[12] One very well known story of betrayal—perhaps the best known of such accounts—is the story of the selling of Joseph to Midianite merchants in Genesis 37, and a strong argument can be made that this story is the basis for the story of the betrayal of Jesus by Judas. In Genesis, it is another Judas—Judah, Yehuda—who betrays a brother, for pieces of silver, to the grief of their father. I suggest that the story of Judas Iscariot as betrayer may well be an adaptation of the story of the act of betrayal by a more famous Judas, Judah or Yehuda son of Jacob, whose name is forever linked to the tribe and territory of Judah and the nature of Jewish identity.

Judas Iscariot, the most provocative character in the drama of Jesus, may have been an historical disciple of Jesus. Plenty of men named Judas were around in the first century, and people named Judas (perhaps like Judas Thomas) were among friends and family members of Jesus. The story of Judas's act of betrayal, however, seems to be literary fiction, composed with the character of Judas son of Jacob in mind. The story of the betrayal of Jesus by Judas makes it sound like Jesus was betrayed by "the Jew," and part of the motivation for the inclusion of such a story in the gospel accounts may be the same as the reason other stories were included that lay the responsibility for the death of Jesus on the Jews—to get Pilate and the Romans off the hook and place the blame for the crucifixion on the Jews. If it is concluded that Judas Iscariot may not be a betrayer of Jesus after all, the story of the death of Jesus is fundamentally changed, and Judas, no longer a betrayer, finally is restored as friend and is redeemed.

The Gospel of Judas survives in Coptic translation as the third text in Codex Tchacos. A brief description of some of the contents of

12. In world literature cf. the story of Melanthius the goatherd, who turned against Odysseus in Homer's *Odyssey* and paid the ultimate price, and the story of Devadatta the cousin of the Buddha, who plotted against the Buddha, unsuccessfully. See Meyer, *Judas*, 139–48; Meyer, *The Gospel of Judas: On a Night with Judas Iscariot*, 79–81.

the Gospel of Judas is found in Irenaeus of Lyon (*Against Heresies* 1.31.1), and although the description is deliberately polemical, it adheres rather closely to the contents of the Coptic version of the Gospel of Judas, even in its indication of the sequence of themes in the narrative. Scholars assume, with good reason, that the Gospel of Judas was originally composed in Greek and translated into Coptic at a later date. The place of composition is unknown. Irenaeus of Lyon published his work *Against Heresies* in the latter part of the second century, and because of the close correspondence between his description of the Gospel of Judas and the Coptic text, we may surmise that Irenaeus was acquainted, to some extent, with the Gospel of Judas in Greek, and hence a date of composition may be suggested not later than sometime around the middle of the second century.

Additional reading: Ehrman, *The Lost Gospel of Judas Iscariot*; Gubar, *Judas: A Biography*; Kasser, Meyer, and Wurst, *The Gospel of Judas* (2nd ed.); Kasser, Meyer, Wurst, and Gaudard, *The Gospel of Judas, Together with the Letter of Peter to Philip, James, and a Book of Allogenes, from Codex Tchacos*; Klassen, *Judas: Betrayer or Friend of Jesus?*; Krosney, *The Lost Gospel*; Krosney, Meyer, and Wurst, "Preliminary Report on New Fragments of Codex Tchacos"; Maccoby, *Judas Iscariot and the Myth of Jewish Evil*; Meyer, *The Gospel of Judas: On a Night with Judas Iscariot*; Meyer, "Jesus, Judas Iscariot, and the *Gospel of Judas*"; Meyer, *Judas*; Paffenroth, *Judas: Images of the Lost Disciple*; Pagels and King, *Reading Judas*; Spong, *Liberating the Gospels: Reading the Bible with Jewish Eyes*.

Translation: The Gospel of Judas

Prologue[1]

The hidden revelatory discourse[2] that Jesus spoke with Judas Iscariot during a period of eight days,[3] up to three days before he celebrated Passover.[4]

Jesus' Signs and Teachings

When he appeared on earth, he performed signs and great wonders for the salvation of humanity. Since some [walked] in the path of righteousness but others wandered in their transgression, the twelve disciples were called.[5]

He began to speak with them about the mysteries that transcend the world and what is going to happen at the end. Time and again he does not appear as himself to his disciples, but you find him among them as a child (?).[6]

Jesus Laughs at the Thanksgiving

Now, one day in Judea he came to his disciples and found them sitting together and practicing their piety. When he [drew] near to his disciples [34] as they were sitting together and giving thanks[7] over the bread, [he] laughed.[8]

The disciples said to him, "Master, why are you laughing at [our] thanksgiving?[9] We have done what is right, haven't we?"

He answered and said to them, "I'm not laughing at you. You are not doing this of your own will but because this is how your god [will be] praised."

They said, "Master, you . . .[10] are the son of our god."[11]

Jesus said to them, "How do you know me? [I'm] telling you the truth, no generation[12] of the people with you will know me."

When his disciples heard this, [they] began getting angry, raging and blaspheming against him in their hearts.

When Jesus saw that they did not understand, [he said] to them, "Why has this confusion led to anger? Your god who is within you and [his powers][13] [35] have become angry together with your souls. [Let] any one of you who is a [strong enough] person bring forward the perfect human and stand before my face."

They all said, "We are strong."

But their spirits did not dare to stand before [him], except for Judas Iscariot. He was able to stand in his presence, yet he could not look him in the eye, but he turned his face away.[14]

Judas [said] to him, "I know who you are and where you have come from. You have come from the immortal aeon[15] of Barbelo,[16] and I am not worthy to utter the name of the one who has sent you."[17]

Jesus Takes Judas Aside

Jesus recognized that Judas[18] was contemplating even more of the things that are lofty, and he said to him, "Step away from the others and I shall explain to you the mysteries of the kingdom, not so that you will go there,[19] but you[20] will experience a great deal of grief. [36] For someone else will take your place, so that the twelve [disciples] will again be complete with their god."[21]

Judas said to him, "When will you tell me these things? And when will the great day of light dawn for [that (?)] generation?"[22]

But when he said this, Jesus left him.

Jesus Again Appears to the Disciples

The next day, in the morning, he [appeared] to his disciples.

They said to him, "Master, where did [you] go and what did you do after you left us?"

Jesus said to them, "I went to another generation, one that is great and holy."

His disciples said to him, "Lord,[23] what is the great and holy generation that is exalted above us but is not present in these aeons?"

When Jesus heard this, he laughed and said to them, "Why are you wondering in your minds about the mighty and holy generation? [37]

[I'm] telling you the truth,
no one born [of] this aeon will behold that [generation],

no angelic host of the stars will rule over that generation,
no person of mortal birth will be able to join it,
because that generation is not from . . .
that has become . . .
the generation of people among [them],
but it is from the generation of the great people,[24]
. . . [none of] the powerful authorities . . . ,
nor any of the powers [of the] aeons,[25]
through which you rule."

When his disciples heard this, each of them was troubled in spirit. They could not say a word.

On another day Jesus came to them, and they said to him, "Master, we had a vision of you, for we had powerful [dreams] last night."

[He said], "Why did [you] . . . and go into hiding?"[26] **[38]**

The Disciples Envision a Temple

They [said, "We] saw a huge house[27] [with a] great altar [in it], and twelve men—they were priests, we think—and a name.[28] And there was a crowd in attendance at that altar,[29] [until] the priests [came and received] the offerings. We [also] were in attendance."

[Jesus] said, "What are [the priests][30] like?"

They said, "[Some] abstain[31] for two weeks. Some sacrifice their own children, others their wives, as they praise and act humbly toward one another. Some sleep with men. Some engage in acts of murder. Some commit all sorts of sins and crimes. The men standing [before] the altar are invoking your [name], **[39]** and that [altar] is filled through all the actions of their sacrifice."[32]

After they said this, they were silent, for they were perplexed.

Jesus Interprets the Vision

Jesus said to them, "Why are you perplexed? I'm telling you the truth, all the priests standing before that altar are invoking my name. I'm also telling you this, my name has been written on this house[33] of the generations of the stars by the human generations. In my name, in a shameful way, they have planted trees with no fruit."[34]

Jesus said to them, "It is you who are presenting the offerings at the altar you have seen. That is the god you worship. The twelve men you have seen—they are you. And the animals you have seen brought in as offerings—they are the crowd you are leading astray [40] at that altar. [Your minister (?)][35] will stand and use my name in this way, and generations of the pious will remain committed to it.[36] After this another man will stand up from [those who are immoral],[37] and another [will] stand up from the child-killers, and another from those who sleep with men, and who abstain,[38] and the rest of the people of impurity, lawlessness, and error. And those who say, 'We are like angels,' they are the stars bringing everything to its fulfillment. For they have said to the human generations, 'Look, god has received your offering through the hands of a priest,'[39] that is, the minister of error. But it is the Lord, the Lord of the universe, who commands. On the last day they will be put to shame." [41]

Jesus said [to them], "Stop [sacrificing animals]. You [offered them up] on the altar, and they are with your stars and your angels, where they already have come to their conclusion. So let them be of no account to you, and let them [be] clear [to you]."

His disciples [said, "Lord], cleanse us from the things . . .[40] we have done through the error of the angels."

Jesus said to them,

"It is impossible [for] rivers (?) . . . .
Nor can a fountain quench the [fire]
of the whole inhabited world.
Nor can a [city's] spring satisfy
all the generations,
except the one that is great and stable.[41]
And a single lamp will not[42] shine
on all the aeons,
except the second generation.[43]
Nor can a baker feed all of creation [42]
under [heaven]."

And [when his disciples heard] this, they said to him, "Lord, help us and save us."[44]

Jesus said to them, "Stop disputing with me. Each one of you has his own star,[45] and [each (?)] of the stars will . . . what is his. . . . I was not sent to the corruptible generation but to the generation that is mighty and incorruptible. For no enemy has ruled [over] that generation, nor any of the stars. I'm telling you the truth, the pillar of fire[46] will fall quickly, and that generation will not be moved[47] [by the (?)][48] stars."

Jesus Again Takes Judas Aside

And when Jesus had [said] this, he left and [took] Judas Iscariot with him. He said to him, "The water [from (?)] the high mountain is from [43] . . . that has not come to . . . [the spring of water] for the tree . . . of this aeon . . . after a time . . . . Rather, this[49] has come to water the paradise of God[50] and the race[51] that will endure, because [this] will not defile the [way of life of] that generation, but [it will last] from eternity to eternity."

Judas said to [him], ". . . ,[52] what fruit does this generation produce?"

Jesus said, "The souls of all human generations will die. When these people, however, complete the time of the kingdom and the spirit leaves them, their bodies will die, but their souls will live on and they will be taken up."[53]

Judas said, "And what will the rest of the human generations do?"

Jesus said, "People cannot [44] sow seed[54] on [rock] and harvest their produce.[55] Likewise, the souls of the [defiled] race,[56] together with corruptible wisdom[57] and the hand that created mortal people, [cannot] ascend to the aeons on high.[58] I'm telling you the [truth, no authority] or angel [or] power will be able to behold those [realms] that [this great], holy generation will [behold]."

After Jesus said this, he left.

Judas Recounts His Own Vision

Judas said, "Master, just as you have listened to all of them, now also listen to me. For I have seen a powerful vision."

When Jesus heard this, he laughed and said to him, "O thirteenth spirit,[59] why are you so excited? Speak up, then, and I shall hear you out."

Judas said to him, "In the vision I saw myself as the twelve disciples were stoning me and [45] persecuting [me harshly]. Then I came to the place where . . . after you. I saw [a house there],[60] and my eyes could not [comprehend] its dimensions. Important people were around it. That house had a single room,[61] and in the midst of the house there was [a crowd] . . . .[62] Master, take me in with these people."

[Jesus] answered and said, "Your star has led you astray, Judas. Further,

No person of mortal birth is worthy
to enter the house you have seen.
That place is kept for the holy.[63]
Neither sun nor moon
will rule there, nor the day,
but they[64] will stand for all time
in the aeon with the holy angels.[65]

"Look, I have told you the mysteries of the kingdom, [46] and I have taught you about the error of the stars, and . . . sent . . . over the twelve aeons."

Judas said, "Master, could it be that my seed is subject to the rulers?"[66]

Jesus answered and said to him, "Come, that I may [speak with you] . . . . . . ,[67] but you[68] will experience a great deal of grief when you see the kingdom and its entire generation."

When Judas heard this, he said to him, "What advantage is there for me that you have set me apart from[69] that generation?"

Jesus answered and said, "You will become the thirteenth, and you will be cursed by the rest of the generations, but you will come to rule over them. In the last days they <will . . .> to you, and you will not ascend (?)[70] up [47] to the holy [generation]."

Jesus Teaches Judas about the Universe

Jesus said, "[Come], that I may teach you about the things . . ."[71] that the human . . . will see.[72] For there is a great and infinite aeon, whose dimensions no angelic generation could see. [In] it is the great invisible [Spirit],[73]

> which no eye of an angel has seen,
> no thought of the mind has grasped,
> nor was it called by any name.[74]

"In that place a luminous cloud appeared.[75] And he[76] said, 'Let an angel come into being as my attendant.'[77]

"And a great angel, the Self-Conceived,[78] God of light, came from the cloud. Four other angels came into being for him, from another cloud, and they served as attendants for the angelic Self-Conceived.[79]

"And the Self-Conceived said, [48] 'Let A[damas][80] come into being,' and it happened [as he said].[81] And he [created] the first luminary to rule over him.[82] And he said, 'Let angels come into being to offer worship,' and myriads without number came to be. And he said, '[Let] an aeon of light come into being,' and it came to be. He established the second luminary [to] rule over it, with myriads of angels without number, to offer worship. This is the way he created the rest of the aeons of light, and he made them to be ruled over. And he created myriads of angels without number to serve them.

Adamas, Luminaries, and Aeons in the Heavens

"Adamas[83] was in the first luminous cloud that no angel could see among all those called 'god.' And he [49] . . . that . . . [after] the image . . . and after the likeness of [this] angel. He made the incorruptible [generation] of Seth[84] appear to the twelve androgynous [luminaries] . . .[85] He made seventy-two luminaries appear in the incorruptible generation, by the will of the Spirit. The seventy-two luminaries in turn made three hundred sixty luminaries appear in the incorruptible generation, by the will of the Spirit, so that their number would be five for each.

"Their Father consists of the twelve aeons of the twelve luminaries, and for each aeon there are six heavens, so that there are seventy-two heavens for the seventy-two luminaries, and for each [50] [of them five] firmaments, [so that there are] three hundred sixty [firmaments]. They were given authority, with a [great] angelic host [without number], for praise and worship, and [in addition] virgin spirits,[86] for praise and [worship] of all the aeons and the heavens and their firmaments.[87]

The Angel and the Rulers

"Now, the multitude of those immortals is called 'cosmos,' that is, corruption,[88] by the Father and the seventy-two luminaries with the Self-Conceived and his seventy-two aeons. There[89] the first human appeared, with his incorruptible powers. This is the aeon that appeared with its generation, in which the cloud of knowledge[90] dwells with the angel called [51] El[91] . . . . . .[92] aeon (?) . . .

"After this [El (?)][93] said, 'Let twelve angels come into being [to] rule over chaos and the [underworld].' And look, out of the cloud appeared an [angel], his face blazing with fire[94] and his countenance fouled with blood.[95] His name was Nebro,[96] which means 'rebel.'[97] Others name him Yaldabaoth. And another angel, Sakla, also came out of the cloud. Then Nebro created six angels, with Sakla, to be attendants, and these produced twelve angels in the heavens, each of them receiving a share in the heavens.[98]

"And the twelve rulers[99] said to the twelve angels, 'Let each of you [52] . . . and let them . . . generation . . . [five][100] angels.'

The first is [S]eth, who is called Christ.[101]
The [second] is Harmathoth, who is [the eye of fire (?)].[102]
The [third] is Galila.
The fourth is Yobel.
The fifth is Adonaios.[103]

These are the five who ruled over the underworld and are the first over chaos.[104]

The Creation of Humanity

"Then Sakla said to his angels, 'Let's create a human being after the likeness and after the image.'[105] And they formed Adam and his wife Eve, who in the cloud is called Zoe.[106] For with this name all the generations seek him, and each of them calls her with their own names. Now, Sakla did not [53] command . . . bringing forth, except . . . among the generations . . . which is . . . . And the [angel] said to him, 'Your life and the lives of your children will last for a limited period of time.'"

Jesus and Judas Discuss the Destiny of Humanity

Judas said to Jesus, "[What] is the length of human life?"

Jesus said, "Why are you concerned that Adam, with his generation, has received his length of life with limits,[107] in the place where he has received his kingdom with limits, along with his ruler?"

Judas said to Jesus, "Does the human spirit die?"

Jesus said, "This is how God commanded Michael to give the spirits of people to them while they are worshiping—as a loan. But the Great One commanded Gabriel to give the spirits to the great generation without a king[108]—the spirit and the soul.[109] For this reason, the rest of the souls [54] . . .

". . . they (?) . . . light . . . chaos . . . seek [after] the spirit within you,[110] which you have made to dwell within this flesh among the generations of angels. But God caused knowledge[111] to be given to Adam and those with him, so that the kings of chaos and the underworld would not lord it over them."

Judas said to Jesus, "So what will those generations do?"

Jesus said, "I'm telling you[112] the truth, the stars are coming to their fulfillment over all of them. When Sakla completes the time assigned for him, their first star will appear with the generations, and what has been mentioned will be fulfilled. Then they will engage in immoral acts[113] in my name and slay their children, [55] and they will . . . evil, and . . . . . .[114] the aeons, bringing their generations and offering them to Sakla. After that [Is]rael[115] will come bringing the twelve tribes of Israel from [Egypt].[116] And [the generations] will all serve Sakla, [also] sinning in my name. And[117] your star will rule over the thirteenth aeon."[118]

And after that Jesus [laughed].

[Judas] said, "Master, why [are you laughing]?"

[Jesus] answered and [said], "I'm not laughing [at you] but at the error of the stars, because these six stars are wandering about with these five warriors, and all of them will perish, with their creatures."[119]

Jesus Speaks of the Baptized and the End of the World

Judas said to Jesus, "Those who have been baptized in your name, then, what will they do?"[120]

Jesus said, "I'm telling [you] the truth, this baptism [56] . . . [in] my name . . . . . .[121] this[122] will destroy the entire generation of the earthly man Adam. Tomorrow[123] they will torment the one who bears me.[124] I'm [telling] you[125] the truth, no hand of mortal human [will] sin against me.

"[I'm] telling you the truth, Judas, those [who] offer sacrifices to Sakla [will] all [die (?)],[126] since . . . upon . . . all of them . . . everything evil.

"But you will exceed all of them.[127] For you will sacrifice the man who bears me.[128]

> Already your horn has been raised,
> and your anger has flared up,
> and your star has passed by,
> and your heart[129] has [grown strong].[130] [57]

"[I'm telling you] the truth, your last . . . and . . .[131] come to be . . . the ministers of the aeon have . . . , and the kings have become weak, and the generations of the angels have grieved, and those who are evil . . . the ruler,[132] since he is overthrown. And then the image[133] of the great generation of Adam will be magnified, for prior to heaven, earth, and the angels, that generation from the aeons exists.[134]

"Look, you have been told everything. Lift up your eyes and

behold the cloud and the light within it and the stars surrounding it. And the star that leads the way, that is your star."[135]

Jesus Ascends

So Judas lifted up his eyes and beheld the luminous cloud. And he[136] entered it. Those standing on the ground heard a voice coming out of the cloud and saying, [58] ". . . great generation . . . image . . . and . . . in (?) . . ."[137]

And Judas saw Jesus no more.

At once there was a commotion among the Jews, greater than (?) . . .[138]

Judas Hands Jesus Over

. . . Their chief priests murmured because [he][139] had gone into the guest room[140] for his prayer. But some scholars were there watching closely in order to seize him during the prayer, for they were afraid of the people, since he was regarded by them all as a prophet.

And they approached Judas and said to him, "What are you doing here? You are Jesus' disciple."

He answered them as they wished.

And Judas received some money and handed him over[141] to them.

The Gospel of Judas[142]

Endnotes

1. Codex Tchacos 3: 33,1—58,29. For the Coptic text, cf. Kasser, Meyer, Wurst, and Gaudard, *The Gospel of Judas, Together with the Letter of Peter to Philip, James, and a Book of Allogenes, from Codex Tchacos*; a preliminary presentation of the new fragments is available in Krosney, Meyer, and Wurst, "Preliminary Report on New Fragments of Codex Tchacos." For a recent edition, cf. Jenott, *The Gospel of Judas: Text, Translation, and Historical Interpretation of the Betrayer's Gospel.* A recent translation has also been published by Iricinschi, Jenott, and Townsend, "Gospel of Judas."

2. Coptic *plogo[s] ethep*. The translation of *ethep* as "hidden," from a suggestion of Louis Painchaud, parallels other tractate incipits, or prologues, for example, the Gospel of Thomas ("These are the hidden sayings . . . ," *naei ne enshaje ethep*). The translation, "The hidden revelatory discourse," may highlight the esoteric nature of the Gospel of Judas and the need to discover the hidden message of the text. The translation "revelatory" is used for the word *apophasis*, which Jacques van der Vliet, Gesine Schenke Robinson, and others prefer to translate as "judgment."

3. Or, "a week." Cf. also the octave, an eight-day festival in the liturgical year.

4. Or, "before his passion."

5. On Jesus calling his disciples, cf. Mark 3:13–19; Matthew 10:1–4; Luke 6:12–16.

6. Coptic *enhrot*. Perhaps read, with Wolf-Peter Funk, "as necessary, at will" (Coptic *enhtor*). On Jesus seen as a child, cf. Secret Book of John II, 2; Revelation of Paul 18; Acts of John 88; Hippolytus, *Refutation of All Heresies* 6.42.2; Gospel of the Savior 13; Gospel of Thomas 4. The word "child" could also be translated "apparition." Some scholars prefer to emend the verb in this sentence, "you find," to read "<they> find."

7. Or, "offering a prayer of thanksgiving," perhaps even "celebrating the eucharist" (Coptic *euereukharisti*).

8. On the laughter of Jesus, see (besides the Gospel of Judas): the Secret Book of John; Wisdom of Jesus Christ III, 91–92; Second Discourse of Great Seth 56; Revelation of Peter 81; Basilides (in Irenaeus of Lyon, *Against Heresies* 1.24.4); perhaps Round Dance of the Cross 96. The Macquarie Coptic magical codex (P. Macquarie I 1, edited by Malcolm Choat and Iain Gardner), which illustrates a number of Sethian motifs, also mentions the laughter of Jesus. Jesus, it is said, came down from the aeons above into this world, found Yaldabaoth, brought him up to the light aeons, and laughed—not with the laughter of a human being but with the laughter of God's son.

9. Or, "eucharist."

10. Hans-Gebhard Bethge and Peter Nagel suggest that this lacuna may be restored to read "O Lord" or "the Lord," thus allowing for two possible translations: "you, [O Lord], are the son of our god," or "you are [the Lord], the son of our god."

11. The disciples profess that Jesus is the son of their own god, who is the creator of this world, but they are mistaken.

12. Coptic *genea*, here and below. This term of Greek origin may also be translated as "race."

13. The restoration "[his powers]" (Coptic *n[efcom]*) is tentative; in his edition, Lance Jenott restores this passage to read "[his stars]" (Coptic *n[efsiou]*).

14. Cf. Gospel of Thomas 46.

15. Or, "eternal realm," here and below.

16. Barbelo is the divine Mother and the first emanation of the divine in a number of Sethian texts, e.g., the Secret Book of John II, 4–5. The name

Barbelo may derive from Hebrew (*b-arb*(*a*)*-Elo*), and it may mean "God in four"—that is, God as known through the tetragrammaton, the ineffable name of God, YHWH.

17. It is Judas Iscariot among the disciples who offers the correct profession of who Jesus is, from a Sethian point of view. On the ineffability of such a profession, cf. Gospel of Thomas 13 and the profession of Judas Thomas. In the context of the Gospel of Thomas, perhaps compare the vision in Gospel of Judas 44–45, in which Judas Iscariot says he sees the other disciples stoning him.

18. Lit., "he."

19. The translation is tentative and the ink traces on the papyrus are faint and difficult to read. The reading of the Coptic ink traces adopted here is *oukh hina je ekebok emau*. An earlier reading of the ink traces of the text (*oun com je ekebok emau*) yielded another translation: "It is possible for you to attain it." Some scholars still prefer the earlier reading.

20. Or, "but that you."

21. This seems to be a reference to the appointment of Matthias to replace Judas in the circle of the disciples according to Acts 1:15–26. It is also possible to restore this passage to refer to "the twelve [elements]," perhaps with the twelve signs of the zodiac in mind.

22. The tentative translation "[that (?)] generation" follows the restoration of Iricinschi, Jenott, and Townsend. Throughout the Gospel of Judas, the phrase "that generation" (Coptic *tgenea etemmau*) refers to the great generation of the people of Seth, i.e., the gnostics. Cf. the phrase "those people" (Coptic *nirome etemmau*) used to refer to the people of Seth elsewhere in Sethian literature, for example in the Revelation of Adam 83.

23. Or, "Master" (Coptic *pjois*).

24. The phrase "the great people" (Coptic *ninoc enrome*) is also used in the Sethian Revelation of Adam 74–75 to describe certain people in the Sethian history of salvation who remain holy and undefiled.

25. Partially restored by Gregor Wurst.

26. This fragmentary section may conceivably be restored to refer to premonitions the disciples experience of the arrest of Jesus in the garden of Gethsemane, and what happens thereafter, when the disciples run for their lives.

27. Or, "building." This apparently refers to the Jewish temple in Jerusalem.

28. Probably thought to be either the name of God or the name of Jesus. Wolf-Peter Funk has suggested that something has been omitted by the scribe, so that the sentence may be thought to have read "and a name <was invoked/ was written on . . .>," or the like.

29. The text inadvertently repeats the phrase "at the altar" (dittography).

30. Or, perhaps, "[the people]."

31. Or, "fast." Here and below, on the suggested wicked actions of some religious folks, perhaps cf. Ezekiel 16:15–22.The Pistis Sophia includes similar accusations, as do other texts with lists of vices.

32. Or, "their deficient actions," "their faulty actions," "their wrong actions"—the Coptic reads *shoot*, which may also be translated "deficiency" and

which functions as a technical term for the deficiency of light in many gnostic texts. If "deficiency" is the preferred translation of *shoot*, there may be a contrast here between fullness and deficiency.

33. The translation "this house" (Coptic *peeiei*) is partially restored by Iricinschi, Jenott, and Townsend.

34. On trees and fruit, cf. also Gospel of Judas 43; Revelation of Adam 76; 85.

35. The restoration "[Your minister (?)]" (Coptic [*petendiako*]*nos*) is tentative, and is proposed by Iricinschi, Jenott, and Townsend; it was previously suggested in the critical edition published by the National Geographic research team. Note the use of the same term *diakonos* a few lines down on the same page. Also possible is "[The great overseer (or bishop)]"—so Johanna Brankaer and Hans-Gebhard Bethge—or, less likely, "[The ruler (or, archon) of this world]."

36. Or, "to him."

37. Or, "[those who fornicate]."

38. Or, "fast." Cf. Gospel of Judas 38.

39. Or, possibly, "priests."

40. Perhaps read "[wickedness]" (with Iricinschi, Jenott, and Townsend).

41. Or, "except the great one, as is its destiny" (Coptic *ettesh*). Perhaps compare, here and below, the description in Sethian literature of the generation of Seth as stable and immovable.

42. Perhaps "cannot" is missing or implied here.

43. The reading is tentative. The translation is based on an understanding of the Coptic as *tme(h)snte engenea*, "the second generation." It may be possible to take *tme* as a form of the verb *temmo*, "nurture," and read "to nurture two generations" (whatever that might mean), or to read *tmes nte engenea*, "the offspring of the generations." The lines on the lower half of page 41 were transcribed by Wolf-Peter Funk from an earlier photograph and edited on the basis of a new photograph of a released fragmentary portion of the text.

44. Restored by Wolf-Peter Funk and Gesine Schenke Robinson.

45. This teaching about people and the stars assigned to them seems to derive from Plato (cf. *Timaeus* 41d–42b). On Judas's star, cf. Gospel of Judas 57.

46. On the pillar of fire, cf., for instance, Exodus 13:21–22.

47. Or, "move."

48. On the tentative restoration "[by the (?)]," cf. Iricinschi, Jenott, and Townsend, and the edition of Jenott.

49. Lit., "he" or "it." The antecedent of the pronoun is unclear. On Seth as the one who brings water, which is likened to a stream of wisdom, compare, with Birger Pearson, Philo of Alexandria, *De Posteritate Caini* ("On the Posterity and Exile of Cain") 36, 49.

50. Cf. Genesis 2:10.

51. Or, "generation" (Coptic [*ge*]*nos*). It may also be possible to restore to read "fruit" (with Iricinschi, Jenott, and Townsend).

52. Perhaps read "[Rabb]i (Coptic [*hrabb*]*ei*, an early reading), "[Tell] me" (Coptic [*tamo*]*ei*, with Wolf-Peter Funk), or the like.

53. The Gospel of Judas seems to understand the human spirit to be the breath of life that animates people and keeps their bodies alive for a time, and the human soul to be the true inner self that allows people of Seth to remain alive and be taken up after their bodies die.

54. The word "seed" is added in the translation for clarification.

55. On this saying, cf. the parable of the sower in Mark 4:1–20; Matthew 13:1–23; Luke 8:4–15; Gospel of Thomas 9.

56. Or, "generation" (Coptic *genos*).

57. Sophia. Here wisdom or Sophia may refer to the personified figure of Wisdom or serve as a more general reference to wisdom. In contrast to a number of other Sethian texts, there is no evidence of an account of the fall of Sophia here in the Gospel of Judas.

58. The organization and presentation of this sentence follows Iricinschi, Jenott, and Townsend.

59. Or, "daimon," or "demon." I prefer to translate the term as "spirit," the most neutral translation. Cf. the role of the spirit or daimon of Socrates as a guiding spirit in Plato's *Symposium*. In the Greco-Roman world a daimon was usually considered an intermediate being, between the human and divine realms. In Jewish and Christian literature, the word "daimon" commonly designates an evil demon, a point emphasized by April DeConick and others. In the Pistis Sophia and elsewhere, Sophia, like Judas, is likened to a daimon. Pseudo-Tertullian states in his work *Against All Heresies* (*Adversus omnes haereses*) 1.2 that Simon Magus is said to have come into this world on behalf of an erring daimon (Latin *daemonem*), who is wisdom (*sapientia*). Further, Irenaeus of Lyon maintains that some second-century gnostics (perhaps Valentinians) compared the figures of Judas and Sophia in terms of their experiences in this world (*Against Heresies* 2.20). In a manner that closely parallels the portrayal of Judas Iscariot in the Gospel of Judas, Sophia in the Pistis Sophia and other texts is likened to a daimon (Coptic *daimon, refshoor*), perhaps as an intermediary being; she is persecuted at the hands of the archons of the twelve aeons; and though long separated from it, she will return to her dwelling place, described as being in "the thirteenth aeon, the place of righteousness." Here, in the Gospel of Judas, Judas is described as the thirteenth, perhaps in part because he is excluded from the group of the twelve disciples.

60. Or, "[in that place]" (restored by Iricinschi, Jenott, and Townsend).

61. This translation follows that of Jacques van der Vliet. Rather than "room," it is also possible to translate this as "roof" (thus, "a single roof," "a thatched roof," even "a <broad> roof"). Iricinschi, Jenott, and Townsend prefer to translate this phrase as "a roof of lightning," and they refer to the similar description of the heavenly house in 1 Enoch. See also the edition of Lance Jenott. On the heavenly house or mansion in the Gospel of John, cf. John 14:1–14.

62. About two lines missing. Judas is speaking the following sentence in his account of the vision.

63. Or, "the saints."

64. The holy.

65. On this description of the heavenly house, cf. the portrayal of the heavenly city in Revelation 21:23. In the Secret Book of John II, 9, the souls of the holy, or the saints, dwell in the third aeon with the third luminary, Daveithai, the place where the offspring of Seth reside.

66. Archons. Or, "Master, surely my seed does not subdue the rulers!"

67. About two lines missing. The clause "so that I may [speak with you]" is partially restored by Iricinschi, Jenott, and Townsend.

68. Or, "but that you."

69. Here the thought may be that Judas is set apart from that generation in the sense of being oppressed in this world of mortality. On Judas being set apart from the disciples, cf. Gospel of Judas 35. Earlier translations by the National Geographic research team, and Elaine Pagels and Karen King, suggested that this preposition might also possibly mean "for" (compare Crum, *A Coptic Dictionary*, 271b–272a). Now most of us prefer the translation "from."

70. Or, "they <will . . .> to you, that you may not ascend." This remains a difficult passage, and the translation I adopt here assumes, with Wolf-Peter Funk and Peter Nagel, that an ancient translator or scribe inadvertently omitted an unknown number of letters, words, or lines. Such an assumption of an ancient textual error, posited in order to explain a difficult reading that defies easy translation, should please no one. Originally the passage was read as follows: *senakauo nekkte epshoi*, "they will curse your ascent." The current reading is this: *se<na . . .* (the verb is assumed to be missing)> *nak auo nekbok epshoi*, "they <will . . .> to you, and you will not ascend." Other readings and translations may prove possible. For example, if the verb *nekbok* is taken to be a conjunctive form, as mentioned by Lance Jenott and others, with hesitation, the translation could be quite different: "and you will ascend."

71. Perhaps restore to read "[mysteries]" (with Iricinschi, Jenott, and Townsend).

72. Here Gregor Wurst suggests the possible restoration "that the human [generation] (Coptic *ge[nea]*) will see." An earlier suggestion proposed that the passage be restored to read "that [no] (*lao[ue]*) person will see" (there are grammatical issues with this restoration). The following cosmogonic revelation is put on the lips of Jesus in the Gospel of Judas, but except for what may be a Christian interpolation on page 52, the revelation seems to be a Hellenistic Jewish composition with a mystical or Sethian perspective. The closest parallels are to be found in the Secret Book of John, the Holy Book of the Great Invisible Spirit, Eugnostos the Blessed, and the Wisdom of Jesus Christ. For gnostic texts that also are secondarily Christianized, compare the Secret Book of John, and the transformation of the Jewish text Eugnostos the Blessed into the Christian Wisdom of Jesus Christ.

73. The highest expression of the divine is frequently called the great invisible Spirit in Sethian texts; cf. Secret Book of John II, 2–3.

74. Cf. 1 Corinthians 2:9; Gospel of Thomas 17; Dialogue of the Savior 140.

75. Compare, perhaps, the place of Barbelo in other Sethian texts (see also Gospel of Judas 35 and the note).

76. Or, "it"—that is, the Spirit.

77. Or, "assistant," "helper," here and below.

78. Autogenes, the Self-Generated, here and below. In Sethian texts the child of the great invisible Spirit is often called Autogenes, the Self-Conceived or Self-Generated. Cf. the Secret Book of John II, 6–7.

79. In Sethian texts four luminaries, usually named Harmozel, Oroiael, Daveithai, and Eleleth, come into existence through the Self-Conceived, Autogenes. Cf., for instance, the Holy Book of the Great Invisible Spirit III, 50–51.

80. Restored by Uwe-Karsten Plisch. Iricinschi, Jenott, and Townsend suggest the reading "an [aeon]" (Coptic o[uaion]); see the edition of Jenott.

81. Restored by Peter Nagel and accepted by Gregor Wurst. An earlier reading, by John Turner, suggested "[the emanation] came to be."

82. Or, "for [him] to rule over."

83. Adamas is Adam, the first human in Genesis, understood here in a Sethian and Platonic fashion as the heavenly archetype and exalted image of humanity. As in Genesis, Adamas is the father of Seth and the generation of Seth. Cf. Secret Book of John II, 8–9.

84. This is Seth son of Adamas, also in the exalted heavenly realm. On Seth, cf. Genesis 4:25–26; 5:3. On Seth being in the likeness and image of Adam in Genesis 5:3, perhaps compare the lines just above the reference to Seth in the Gospel of Judas.

85. The reading "androgynous" (Coptic enhoout[shi]me) is suggested by Iricinschi, Jenott, and Townsend. Less likely is "the twelve [luminaries], the twenty-four . . ." (Coptic enjout[a]fte . . .).

86. Cf. close parallels in Eugnostos the Blessed III, 88–89; Wisdom of Jesus Christ III, 113; On the Origin of the World 105–6.

87. Cf. Eugnostos the Blessed III, 83–84.

88. Coptic phthora. Compare, with Lance Jenott, Philo of Alexandria, *De Aeternitate Mundi* ("On the Eternity of the World") 9, on the Stoic view of the cosmos, which, depending on the point of view, may be described as either eternal or corruptible (*phthora*).

89. I.e., in the cosmos.

90. Gnosis.

91. Or, "El[eleth]," or even "El[el]." Cf. Eleleth in other Sethian texts; a number of scholars prefer the reading "El[eleth]" here in the Gospel of Judas as well. El is an ancient Middle Eastern name for God, and Eleleth is considered one of the luminaries in Sethian texts. On the use of shorter forms of names, without honorific or other suffixes, compare Nebro, later in the text, and Addon (in contrast to Ad(d)onaios) within the tractate James in Codex Tchacos. On Eleleth, compare the angel who gives revelation to Norea at the conclusion of the text entitled the Nature of the Rulers (93). Eleleth takes on a creative role in the Sethian text Three Forms of First Thought (39). The role of Eleleth in the

Holy Book of the Great Invisible Spirit III, 56 is described in terms close to the language of the Gospel of Judas.

92. Almost two lines missing.

93. "[El (?)]," "[Eleleth (?)]," or perhaps "[Elel (?)]" follows the suggestion of Iricinschi, Jenott, and Townsend, connects with the previous reference to El, Elel, or Eleleth, and parallels the role of Eleleth in Three Forms of First Thought and the Holy Book of the Great Invisible Spirit.

94. On the creator God with eyes flashing, cf. Secret Book of John II, 10.

95. On Sophia of matter defiled with blood, cf. Holy Book of the Great Invisible Spirit III, 56–57.

96. On Nebruel, cf. Holy Book of the Great Invisible Spirit III, 57. Nebroel is also referred to as a female figure in Manichaean texts. In the Gospel of Judas Nebro is referred to without the honorific suffix -el. Here Nebro is said to mean "rebel," and Nebro may be related to Nimrod (Greek *Nebrod*), the legendary character in ancient Middle Eastern traditions (cf. Genesis 10:8–12; 1 Chronicles 1:10). Scholars have suggested that the name Nimrod may be connected to the Hebrew word for "rebel."

97. Or, "apostate."

98. The names Yaldabaoth and Sakla (or Saklas) are well known names of the demiurge in Sethian and other texts. Both names derive from Aramaic or Hebrew. Yaldabaoth means "child of chaos" or "child of (S)abaoth," Sakla(s) means "fool." The description of the twelve angels, each with a share in the heavens, probably refers to the twelve signs of the zodiac.

99. Archons.

100. Restored by Peter Nagel.

101. Here, rather than "[S]eth," Turner and DeConick read "[Ath]eth," and rather than "Christ" (*kh*(*risto*)*s*), Turner and DeConick read "the good one" (*kh*(*resto*)*s*), as does Lance Jenott in his edition. Jacques van der Vliet hypothesizes that a scribe mistakenly read the word *krios* (Aries, the Ram, as the heavenly constellation), which was originally in the text, as *khristos*. The attempt on the part of some scholars to read *pej*(*oei*)*s*, "the lord," rather than *pekh*(*risto*)*s*, "Christ," is made difficult by the form of the definite article (*pe*-) typically used with a noun beginning with two consonants. The restoration of the name "[S]eth" is made on the basis of the existing ink traces, the amount of space available, and the connection with "Christ." In his edition Jenott suggests, among other possibilities, "[Ya]oth, who is called the good one."

102. Here Jenott, in his edition, restores to read "Harmathoth, who is [the eye of fire]," and DeConick and Turner suggest the reading "Harmathoth, who is [the evil eye]." In the present translation I opt, tentatively, for Jenott's restoration. On the latter reading, cf. Secret Book of John II, 10 ("The second is Harmas, who is the jealous [or, evil, Coptic *koh*)] eye"). The former reading, "[the eye of fire (Coptic *koht*)]," is attested in other editions of the Secret Book of John.

103. Cf. Secret Book of John II, 10–11; Holy Book of the Great Invisible Spirit III, 57–58. In the list in the Gospel of Judas, the second angelic power

is Harmathoth; in the Secret Book of John and the Holy Book of the Great Invisible Spirit, the first two are Athoth and Harmas. The two names seem to have been conflated in the Gospel of Judas, as Harmathoth, to allow for the reference to Christ in the previous line. The apparent correlation of Seth and Christ as the first angelic power is unusual in the context of other Sethian texts, although the identification of Seth and Christ certainly is not. In Christian Sethian texts it is usual to see Christ as an incarnation or manifestation of Seth. Cf. Holy Book of the Great Invisible Spirit III, 63–64; Three Forms of First Thought 50.

104. Or, "first of all over chaos."

105. Cf. Genesis 1:26. This passage is interpreted in gnostic texts and particularly in Sethian texts to explain how human beings both reflect the image of divinity and also resemble the features of the cosmic powers. The Secret Book of John describes how the image of divine forethought (or heavenly Adamas) seen by Yaldabaoth and the archons becomes the basis for the creation of a human being after the image of God and with a likeness to the archons themselves (II, 15). Here in the Gospel of Judas (48) cf. the comparable place of Adamas as heavenly archetype and image of humanity.

106. Zoe, which means "life," is the Greek name for Eve.

107. Here and below this phrase reads, literally, "in a number." The second instance of this phrase could conceivably be a case of dittography.

108. Or, "the great generation with no ruler over it," "the great kingless generation"—that is, the seed or offspring of Seth. Cf. the description of the offspring of Seth in the Revelation of Adam as "the generation without a king" (82).

109. God—perhaps the god of this world?—gives the spirit of life to people, through the archangel Michael, as a loan, but the Great One gives spirit and soul to people, through the archangel Gabriel, as a gift. Cf. Genesis 2:7, on God breathing the breath of life into the human being, and the Sethian interpretation of the divine subterfuge leading to the empowerment of Adam in the Secret Book of John (II, 19).

110. Plural.

111. Gnosis.

112. Plural.

113. Or, "fornicate."

114. Almost three lines missing.

115. "[Is]rael" or "[Ist]rael"? Compare the name as it appears on magical amulets. See Bonner, *Studies in Magical Amulets, Chiefly Graeco-Egyptian*, 281.

116. The restoration of "[Egypt]" is suggested by Louis Painchaud. In this context, which calls to mind the story of the exodus from Egypt, compare the reference to the pillar of fire in Gospel of Judas 42. The present section seems to provide an abbreviated Sethian interpretation of the history of Israel, from early periods until the time of Jesus.

117. Here the word "and" may be repeated (a case of dittography).

118. On the thirteenth aeon as the place over which the star of Judas will rule, compare the references to the thirteen aeons and the God of the thirteen aeons—the demiurge, the creator of this mortal world below—in the Holy Book of the Great Invisible Spirit (III, 63) and Zostrianos (4), and thirteen kingdoms in the Revelation of Adam (77–82). The phrase "thirteenth aeon" shows up more than forty times in the Pistis Sophia (and it also is to be found in the Books of Jeu), where it is "the place of righteousness" located above the twelve aeons and the heavenly home of the twenty-four luminaries—including Sophia, who calls the thirteenth aeon "my dwelling place." In the literature of antiquity and late antiquity, the thirteenth aeon can occupy a place just above the twelve (who are often considered to be the signs of the zodiac), on the border of the infinite—a place, it may be, between the world of mortality below and the world of the divine on high, and as such it is a place with a certain ambivalence. According to the Pistis Sophia, Sophia, straining to ascend to the light above, is deceived and comes down from the thirteenth aeon, descending through the twelve aeons to "chaos" below. Here in this world she is oppressed, and the powers of the world, including lion-faced Yaldabaoth, seek to rob her of the light within her. For a time, she is prevented from leaving the place of her oppression. In the midst of her suffering, Pistis Sophia—the wisdom of God weakened and languishing in this world, reflective of the soul of the gnostic trapped here below—cries for salvation, and eventually her cry is heard (1.50). Much of the reflection upon the thirteenth aeon in the Pistis Sophia recalls the Gospel of Judas and the place of Judas Iscariot in the Gospel of Judas.

119. The wandering stars are usually understood to be the planets. Here the six wandering stars are probably the five known planets (Mercury, Venus, Mars, Jupiter, Saturn) and the moon.

120. The place and nature of baptism is significant in Sethian gnostic texts, and a clear distinction is made between the baptism in the emerging orthodox church and Sethian baptism. On Sethian baptism, cf. the Holy Book of the Great Invisible Spirit (III, 63–67).

121. Almost three lines missing.

122. Lit., "he" or "it." The antecedent of the pronoun is unclear.

123. Friday, i.e., Good Friday, the day of crucifixion.

124. Or, in the passive, "Tomorrow the one who bears me will be tormented." On the image, here and below, of the one who "bears" Jesus, compare Jenott's observation, in his edition, that this language recalls the traditional philosophical description of the body supporting or carrying the soul. Thus, in his *Timaeus*, Plato presents the body as that which "bears" a person's head, which in turn houses the soul.

125. Plural.

126. The restoration of these lines is somewhat uncertain; a verb in a future tense is expected in connection with those who offer sacrifices to Sakla. The restored reading adopted here, tentatively, is "[senam]ou terou." Other similar readings are possible.

127. Probably the other disciples. Precisely how and why Judas will exceed the others remain uncertain. Perhaps it is because Judas is not among those who offer sacrifices to Sakla and die. Perhaps it is because Judas plays a more prominent role in bringing about the apocalyptic events that will change the world forever. Perhaps it is because, as Irenaeus of Lyon says, only Judas knew the truth and accomplished the mystery of the betrayal. On Jesus telling Judas, in the context of the New Testament discussion of the betrayal, "What you are going to do, do quickly," cf. John 13:27.

128. The one whom Judas will "sacrifice" is not the spiritual Jesus but rather the mortal body Jesus has been using. This act on the part of Judas, described by Irenaeus as the "mystery of the betrayal," leads to the apocalyptic events described in the following lines. On the true, spiritual Jesus escaping crucifixion, compare the Second Discourse of Great Seth, the Nag Hammadi Revelation of Peter, Basilides (in Irenaeus of Lyon, *Against Heresies* 1.24.4), and other sources.

129. Or, "mind."

130. These lines recall 1 Samuel 2:1 (the song of Hannah—suggested to me by Tage Petersen). The song of Hannah is employed elsewhere in early Christian literature, and it served as a model for the Magnificat of Mary in Luke 1. The line about the star of Judas coheres well with the astronomical/astrological emphasis of the Gospel of Judas.

131. In his edition Jenott restores to read "your last [days have come]. And . . . ."

132. Archon.

133. Or, "fruit," or "place" (suggested by Iricinschi, Jenott, and Townsend).

134. Everything that is earthly and heavenly is undone, as Irenaeus states in his brief synopsis of the Gospel of Judas, but those of that generation—of "the image of the great generation of Adam"—will be glorified. In this regard Lance Jenott concludes, in his edition, that the Gospel of Judas interprets the passion of Jesus as an act of triumph over the malevolent powers of the world, and Jesus appears as *Christus Victor*. While I appreciate Jenott's positive understanding of the death of Jesus in the Gospel of Judas as an event that brings about victory over the cosmic powers, I suggest that the Gospel of Judas, in good Sethian fashion, stresses the primacy of the spiritual, divine nature of Jesus.

135. Jesus, the new fragments confirm, is about to ascend to a luminous cloud, and the stars of the disciples surround the cloud as witnesses, with the star of Judas in the lead.

136. Here the pronoun refers to Jesus (so also Sasagu Arai, Birger Pearson, Gesine Schenke Robinson, and others). In the Gospel of Judas it is Jesus who is transfigured and ascends to the luminous realm. The spiritual person of Jesus returns to the light above, and his fleshly body that is left behind in this world below is handed over to the authorities to be crucified. On the transfiguration of Jesus, cf. the accounts in the New Testament gospels and the Book of Allogenes 61–62ff.; on the ascension of Jesus, cf. Acts 1 and other texts.

137. The content of the revelation from the voice out of the cloud is uncertain, on account of the fragmentary nature of the text, but the words preserved ("great generation," "image") suggest a positive statement about those who are saved.

138. The reference, though fragmentary, to a "commotion among the Jews" may anticipate the crucifixion of the earthly body of Jesus and the subsequent eschatological events. Compare, perhaps, the passion narrative in the Gospel of Matthew, with its apocalyptic elements.

139. Or, "[they]."

140. Mark 14:14 and Luke 22:11 use the same word for "guest room" (*kataluma*).

141. Here the Coptic verb for "hand over" is *paradidou* (from the Greek *paradidonai*), as in the New Testament gospels and the letters of Paul.

142. Coptic *peuaggelion enioudas*, "The Gospel of Judas" (not "The Gospel according to Judas").

5

EPILOGUE

Gospel of the Redeemed—Draft Chapters
in a Gospel of Wisdom, with Restored Disciples

In this epilogue I offer a rhetorical exercise in which a gospel account, a Gospel of the Redeemed, is provided with the arguments
of this book in mind. This gospel account is not meant to recre-
ate any ancient gospel or to suggest scholarly ways in which early
Christian gospels may be analyzed and edited. Rather, I present a
first effort at imagining what a familiar gospel account might look
like if it emphasizes the wisdom of Jesus and portrays doubting
Thomas, Mary the repentant woman, and Judas the betrayer in a
new and different way. What is intended is a presentation of a gospel of wisdom, with salvific features of the cross and resurrection
deemphasized. I have based the account given here on passages
from the earliest New Testament gospel, the Gospel of Mark, and
I have translated and paraphrased the Markan passages in what I
judge to be an appropriate way for the purposes of this rhetorical
exercise. I have included part of the Sermon on the Mount from the
Gospel of Matthew (and the sayings gospel Q) as reflective of the
wisdom sayings of Jesus the Jewish[1] sage and storyteller. Into the
account I have also inserted selections, longer and shorter, from
other early Christian texts discussed in this book, particularly the

1. Or perhaps more accurately, "Judean," here and below.

Gospels of Thomas, Mary, and Judas, in order to show these three disciples no longer marginalized but rather restored to a position of loyalty. The result is a composite narrative, derived from a variety of sources, a narrative that retells a story with an engaging tale of a Jewish man of wisdom and a fresh vision of Jesus and his disciples.

Translation: Gospel of the Redeemed

Prologue

These are the words the living Jesus spoke and Judas Thomas, Mary Magdalene, and others recorded. And he said, "Whoever discovers what these sayings mean will not taste death."

Jesus said,

Seek and do not stop seeking
until you find. When you find,
you will be troubled. When you are troubled,
you will be astonished and will reign over all,
and you will rest.[1]

The Beginning of the Story of Jesus

The story of the good news of Jesus Christ begins with what is written in Isaiah the prophet:

Look, I send my messenger before your face
to prepare the way for you.
The voice of one shouting in the desert,
"Prepare the way of the Lord,
make his paths straight."

John the baptizer appeared in the desert proclaiming baptism for repentance and forgiveness of sins. All those from the countryside of Judea and all the people of Jerusalem went out to him and were baptized by him in the Jordan River, and they confessed their sins. Now, John wore clothing made of camel's hair and had a leather belt around his waist, and he ate locusts and wild honey. He began his proclaiming by saying, "Someone is coming after me who is mightier than me, and I am not worthy to bend over and untie his sandal straps. I have baptized you with water, but he will baptize you with holy spirit."

At that time Jesus came from Nazareth in Galilee and was baptized by John in the Jordan. And at once as he came up from the water, he saw the skies open and the spirit coming down on him like a dove, and a voice came from the skies, "You are my child, whom I love, and I am well pleased with you."

Then Jesus looked around and said, "From Adam to John the baptizer, among those born of women, no one is greater than John the baptizer, so that his eyes should not be averted. But I have said, whoever among you becomes a child will know the kingdom and become greater than John."[2]

At once the spirit drove Jesus out into the desert, and he was in the desert for forty days, put to the test by Satan. And he was among wild beasts, and angels took care of him.

After John was arrested, Jesus came to Galilee proclaiming the good news of God and saying, "The time is up and the kingdom of God is near. Repent and believe in the good news."

He added, "If your leaders tell you, 'Look, the kingdom is in heaven,' then the birds of heaven will precede you. If they say to you, 'It's in the sea,' then the fish will precede you. Rather, the kingdom is inside you and it is outside you. When you know yourselves, then you will be known, and you will understand that you are children of the living Father. But if you do not know yourselves, then you dwell in poverty and you are poverty."[3]

And Jesus laughed.[4]

And as he was walking along by the Sea of Galilee, he saw Simon and Andrew, brother of Simon, casting their nets into the sea. They were fishermen. Jesus said to them, "Follow me and I'll get you to fish for people." And at once they left their nets behind and followed him.

A little farther on he saw James son of Zebedee and John his brother mending their nets in their boat. And at once he called to them, and they left father Zebedee in the boat with the hired hands and followed him.

Also there was Mary, a woman of Magdala, a town on the sea with a fishing industry. Jesus called to her, and at once she left her friends and family behind and followed Jesus.

They went to Capernaum, and at once on the Sabbath he entered the synagogue and began to teach. They were astonished at his teaching, for he would teach them as a person of authority, and not like their scholars.

And at once in their synagogue there was a man with an unclean spirit, and it shouted out, "Jesus of Nazareth, what do you want with us? Have you come to destroy us? I know who you are. You are the holy man of God."

But Jesus shouted back at it and said, "Shut up and come out of him!"

The unclean spirit brought convulsions upon the man, and it uttered a loud scream and came out of him. And they all were astonished and asked each other, "What's this? It's a new sort of teaching! He gives orders with authority even to unclean spirits, and they obey him." And at once his reputation spread around everywhere through the whole region of Galilee.

And at once they left the synagogue and went into the house of Simon and Andrew, with James and John. Simon's mother-in-law was sick with a fever, and at once they told him about her. So he came up to her, took her by the hand, and raised her up. The fever left her, and she began to take care of them.

That night, when the sun went down, they brought to him all the sick and demon possessed. The whole town was crowding around the door. And he healed many who were sick with different diseases, and he drove out many demons. He wouldn't let the demons speak, because they knew who he was.

The next morning, while it was still dark, he got up and went out to a place of solitude, and there he prayed. And Simon and those with him caught up with him. When they found him, they said to him, "Everyone is looking for you."

He said to them, "Let's go to the neighboring towns so I can preach there as well. That's what I came for."

And so he went all around Galilee preaching in their synagogues and driving out demons.

Then a man with a skin disease came up to him. He fell on his knees, and begged him and said, "If you want to, you can make me clean."

Jesus was filled with compassion. He reached out his hand and touched him, and said to him, "I do want to. You're clean."

At once the skin disease disappeared, and he was made clean. And Jesus gave him strict orders and sent him away at once, and said to him, "Don't say anything to anyone. But go, have a priest examine you, and then offer for your cleansing what Moses ordered to be done as a proof to the people."

But he left and began to talk to everyone and spread the news, so that Jesus could no longer enter a town openly. He stayed in the countryside, and people came to him from everywhere.[5]

The Disciples around Jesus

Jesus went up on a hill and called those he wished, and they came to him. He formed a group of young men and women to be with him, and to be sent out to preach and have authority to cast out demons:

> Mary of Magdala, called Mary Magdalene,
> who was a beloved disciple,
> Simon, whom he nicknamed Peter,
> Andrew, his brother,
> James son of Zebedee,
> John, his brother,
> the two he nicknamed Boanerges,
> which means "sons of thunder,"
> Salome,
> and another Mary, Martha, and Arsinoe,
> with Philip, Levi, and Judas Thomas,
> who was called the Twin,
> Judas Iscariot,
> whom Jesus trusted with the common purse,[6]
> and a few others.[7]

When Jesus came to Salome and called her, she said, "Who are you, mister? You have climbed onto my couch and eaten from my table as if you are from someone."

Jesus said to her, "I am one who comes from what is whole. I was given from the things of my Father."

Salome answered, "I am your disciple."[8]

To Judas Thomas Jesus said, "You are my twin and true friend. Since you are to be called my brother, it is not fitting for you to be ignorant of yourself. Indeed, already you have obtained knowledge, and you will be called one who knows oneself."[9]

Later the disciples gathered together and said to Jesus, "Your brothers and your mother are standing outside."

He said to them, "The men and women here who do the will of my Father are my brothers and sisters and mother. They are the ones who will enter the kingdom of my Father."[10]

Jesus paused, and he looked at his disciples and said, "Compare me to something and tell me what I am like."

Simon Peter said to him, "You are like a just messenger."

Matthew said to him, "You are like a wise philosopher."

Judas Thomas said to him, "Teacher, my mouth is utterly incapable of saying what you are like."

Jesus said, "I'm not your teacher. Because you have drunk, you are intoxicated from the bubbling spring I have tended."

And he took him and withdrew, and spoke three sayings to him.

When Judas Thomas came back to his companions, they asked him, "What did Jesus say to you?"

Judas Thomas said to them, "If I tell you one of the sayings he spoke to me, you will pick up rocks and stone me, and fire will come out of the rocks and consume you."[11]

Judas Iscariot said to Jesus, "Judas Thomas speaks well. As for me, I know who you are and where you have come from. You have come from the immortal realm above, and I am not worthy to utter the name of the one who has sent you."[12]

Jesus said to them, "Right you are, Judas. And whoever drinks from my mouth will become like me. I myself shall become that person, and the hidden things will be revealed to that one."[13]

The Wisdom of the Teacher

Jesus said to Judas Iscariot and the other disciples, "Come, that I may teach you about the things that no human will see. For there

is a great and infinite realm, whose dimensions no angelic generation could see. In it is the great invisible spirit,

> which no eye of an angel has seen,
> no thought of the mind has grasped,
> nor was it called by any name."[14]

Jesus went on, "When you see one not born of woman, fall on
your faces and worship. That is your Father."[15]

Jesus saw the crowds coming to him, and so he went up a hill
and sat down, and his disciples came to him. And he opened his
mouth and began to teach them, and he said,

> Blessings on the poor in spirit,
> for theirs is the kingdom of heaven.
> Blessings on those who grieve,
> for they will be comforted.
> Blessings on the gentle,
> for they will inherit the earth.
> Blessings on those who hunger and thirst for justice,
> for they will be fed.
> Blessings on the merciful,
> for they will be treated mercifully.
> Blessings on those with clean hearts,
> for they will see God.
> Blessings on those who work for peace,
> for they will be called God's children.
> Blessings on those who are oppressed for the sake of justice,
> for theirs is the kingdom of heaven.
> Blessings on you when people insult you
> and oppress you
> and tell all kinds of evil lies about you
> on account of me.
> Rejoice and be glad,
> for your reward is great in the heavens.
> That is how they oppressed the prophets
> who came before you.

You are the salt of the earth.
But if salt loses its saltiness,
how can it become salty again?
Then it is good for nothing
except to be thrown out
and trampled by people.

You are the light of the world.
A city set on a hilltop cannot be hidden.
Nor do people light a lamp
and put it under a basket,
but on a lamp stand,
and it gives light to everyone in the house.
That is how your light should shine before people,
that they may see your good deeds
and praise your Father in the heavens.

So I'm telling you,
Unless your justice is greater
than that of the scholars and Pharisees,
you will never enter the kingdom of heaven.

You have heard people were told,
An eye for an eye
and a tooth for a tooth.
But I'm telling you,
Do not fight back against someone evil.
If someone slaps you on the right cheek,
turn to the person the other also.
If someone wants to sue you and take your shirt,
let the person have your coat also.
And if someone compels you to go one mile,
go with the person a second mile.
Give to one who begs from you,
and do not refuse one who wants to borrow from you.

The Gospels of the Marginalized

You have heard people were told,
You must love your neighbor,
and you must hate your enemy.
But I'm telling you,
Love your enemies,
and pray for those who oppress you,
that you may be children
of your Father in the heavens.
Your Father makes the sun rise
on the evil and the good,
and makes it rain
on the just and the unjust,
For if you love those who love you,
what reward should you get?
Even tax collectors do as much, don't they?
And if you greet only your friends,
what is so special about that?
Even gentiles do as much, don't they?
So be complete,
as your heavenly Father is complete.

Do not store away for yourselves treasures on earth,
where moths and bugs devour
and where robbers break in and steal.
But store away for yourselves treasures in heaven,
where neither moths nor bugs devour
and where robbers do not break in or steal.
For where your treasure is
your heart will also be found.

The eye is the body's lamp.
So if your eye is healthy,
your whole body will be enlightened,
but if your eye is sick,
your whole body will be darkened.
And if the light within you is darkness,
how dark it is!

No one can serve two masters.
For a person will either hate one and love the other,
or be loyal to one and despise the other.
You cannot serve God and wealth.

That is why I'm telling you,
do not worry about your life,
what you will eat or what you will drink,
or about your body,
what you will wear.
Isn't life more than food,
and the body more than clothing?
Look at the birds of heaven.
They do not plant or harvest or store in barns,
and your heavenly Father feeds them.
You are worth more than they, aren't you?
Can any of you add an hour to your life
by worrying?

And why worry about clothing?
Observe the wild lilies,
how they do not prepare or work or spin.
But I'm telling you,
Not even Solomon at the peak of his glory
was decked out like one of them.
If that is how God clothes the wild grass,
which is here today
and tomorrow is tossed into an oven,
how much more will God clothe you,
you who have so little trust!

So do not worry and say,
What shall we eat,
or what shall we drink,
or what shall we wear?
All this is what the gentiles seek.

For your heavenly Father knows you need all this.
Seek God's kingdom and God's justice first,
and all this will be yours as well.

So do not worry about tomorrow,
for tomorrow can worry about itself.
Each day's trouble is enough for the day.

Do not judge, that you may not be judged.
For the judgment you give
will be the judgment you get,
and the standard you use
will be the standard used on you.
Why do you see a splinter in your friend's eye,
but miss a log in your own eye?
Or how can you say to your friend,
Let me take the splinter out of your eye,
when, look, there is a log in your own eye?
You phony,
first take the log out of your own eye,
and then you will be able to see well enough
to take the splinter out of your friend's eye.

Do not give what is holy to dogs,
and do not throw your pearls to pigs,
or else they may trample them underfoot
and turn and attack you.

Ask and it will be given to you,
seek and you will find,
knock and the door will be opened for you.
For everyone who asks receives,
and everyone who seeks finds,
and for one who knocks
the door will be opened.
Or is there a person among you

who will serve a stone
if your child asks for bread?
Or will serve a snake
if your child asks for fish?
So if you, flawed as you are,
know how to give good gifts to your children,
how much more will your Father in the heavens
give what is good to those who ask!

So in everything,
act toward others
the way you want others to act toward you.

When Jesus had finished these sayings, the crowds were astonished at his teaching. For he, unlike their scholars, was teaching them as a person of authority.[16]

Parables and Stories of the Kingdom

Jesus taught the disciples and others many things in parables and stories.[17]

And he said, "Humankind is like a wise fisherman who cast his net into the sea and drew it up from the sea full of small fish. Among them the wise fisherman found a fine large fish. He threw all the small fish back into the sea and with no difficulty chose the large fish."[18]

Again Jesus said, "Look, the sower went out, took a handful of seeds, and scattered them. Some fell on the road, and birds came and pecked them up. Others fell on rock, and they did not take root in the soil and did not produce heads of grain. Others fell on thorns, and they choked the seeds and worms devoured them. And others fell on good soil, and it brought forth a good crop, yielding sixty per measure and one hundred twenty per measure."[19]

The disciples said to Jesus, "Tell us what the kingdom of heaven is like."

He said to them, "It is like a mustard seed. It is the tiniest of seeds, but when it falls on prepared soil, it produces a large plant and becomes a shelter for birds of heaven."[20]

Mary Magdalene said to Jesus, "What are your disciples like?"

He said, "They are like children living in a field that is not theirs. When the owners of the field come, they will say, 'Give our field back to us.' The children take off their clothes in front of them to give it back, and they return their field to them."[21]

Mary herself replied,

The wickedness of each day is sufficient.
Workers deserve their food.
Disciples resemble their teachers.

She said this as a woman who understood everything.[22]

Then Jesus to her, "Well done, Mary. You are more blessed than all women on earth."[23]

And Jesus told another story: "The kingdom of the Father is like someone who had good seed. His enemy came at night and sowed weeds among the good seed. The person did not let them pull up the weeds but said to him, 'No, or you might go to pull up the weeds and pull up the wheat along with them.' For on harvest day the weeds will stand out and will be pulled up and burned."[24]

Jesus said, "There was a rich man who was very wealthy. He said, 'I shall invest my money so that I may sow, reap, plant, and fill my storehouses with produce. Then I'll lack nothing.' This is what he was thinking in his heart, but that very night he died."[25]

Jesus said, "A person was receiving guests. When he prepared the dinner, he sent his servant to invite the guests.

"The servant went to the first and said, 'My master invites you.'

"That person said, 'Some merchants owe me money. They are coming tonight. I must go and give them instructions. Please excuse me from dinner.'

"The servant went to another and said, 'My master has invited you.'

"He said to the servant, 'I have bought a house and I've been called away for a day. I have no time.'

"The servant went to another and said, 'My master invites you.'

"He said to the servant, 'My friend is to be married and I am to arrange the banquet. I can't come. Please excuse me from dinner.'

"The servant went to another and said, 'My master invites you.'

"He said to the servant, 'I have bought an estate and I am going to collect rent. I can't come. Please excuse me.'

"The servant returned and said to his master, 'Those whom you invited to dinner have asked to be excused.'

"The master said to his servant, 'Go out on the streets and bring back whomever you find for dinner.'"[26]

Jesus said, "A usurer owned a vineyard and rented it to some tenant farmers to work it, and from them he would collect its produce. He sent his servant so that the farmers would give the servant the produce of the vineyard. They seized, beat, and nearly killed his servant, and the servant returned and told his master. His master said, 'Perhaps he did not know them.' He sent another servant, and the farmers beat that one as well. Then the master sent his son and said, 'Perhaps they will show my son some respect.' Since the farmers knew the son was the heir to the vineyard, they seized him and killed him."[27]

Jesus said, "The kingdom of the Father is like a merchant who owned a supply of merchandise and then found a pearl. The merchant was smart. He sold his goods and bought the single pearl for himself."[28]

Jesus said, "The kingdom of the Father is like a woman. She took a little yeast, hid it in dough, and made large loaves of bread."[29]

Jesus said, "The kingdom of the Father is like a woman carrying a jar full of meal. While she was walking along a distant road, the handle of the jar broke and the meal spilled behind her along the road. She did not know it. She noticed no problem. When she reached her house, she put the jar down and found it was empty."[30]

Jesus said, "The kingdom of the Father is like a person who wanted to put a powerful person to death. While at home he drew his sword and thrust it into the wall to find out whether his hand would go in. Then he killed the powerful person."[31]

Jesus said, "The kingdom is like a shepherd who had a hundred sheep. One of them, the largest, went astray. He left the ninety-nine and searched for the one until he found it. After he had gone to this trouble, he said to the sheep, 'I love you more than the ninety-nine.'"[32]

Jesus said, "The kingdom is like a person who had a treasure hidden in his field. He did not know it, and when he died, he left it to his son. The son did not know about it. He took over the field and sold it. The buyer went plowing, discovered the treasure, and began to lend money at interest to whomever he wished."[33]

Jesus said,

It is impossible for rivers to flow for all.
Nor can a fountain quench the fire
of the whole inhabited world.
Nor can a city's spring satisfy
all the generations.
And a single lamp will not shine
on all the realms.
Nor can a baker feed all of creation
under heaven.[34]

Jesus added, "If you have ears to hear, you should hear."[35]

The Last Days of Jesus

After Jesus said these things, he welcomed all of them and said, "Peace be with you; receive my peace. Take care that no one deceives you by saying, 'Look, here,' or 'Look, there.' The child of humanity is within you. Follow that. Those who seek it will find it. Go out and preach the message of good news about the kingdom. Do not make any rules other than what I have given you, and do not lay down law, as the lawgiver has done, or you will be bound by it."[36]

Then Jesus and his disciples arose and set out for Jerusalem. When they approached the city, near Bethphage and Bethany at the Mount of Olives, Jesus sent off two of his disciples and said to them, "Go into the village across the way, and at once, as you enter it, you'll find a colt tied up, one that never before has been ridden. Untie it and bring it over here. If anyone asks you, 'Why are you doing this?' say to them, 'The master needs it, and he will return it at once.'"

They went out and found a colt tied up by the door out on the street, and they untied it. The people standing there said to them, "What are you doing, untying that colt?" They responded just as Jesus had told them, so the people left them alone.

They brought the colt to Jesus, and they threw their garments on it, and got up on it. And many people spread their garments out on the road, and others threw out leafy branches cut from the fields. Those who were leading the way and those who were following called out,

Hosanna!
Blessings on the one who comes in the name of the Lord.
Blessings on the coming kingdom of our father David.
Hosanna in the highest!

And he entered the city of Jerusalem and went into the Temple, and he looked around at everything. And he began to throw out those involved in buying and selling in the Temple, and he overturned the tables of the money-changers and the chairs of the pigeon-sellers. He wouldn't let anyone carry anything through the Temple. And he lectured them and said to them, "Isn't this written?

My house shall be called a house of prayer for all nations.
But you have turned it into a den of thieves."

Some of the leaders heard this, and they looked for a way to destroy him. For they were afraid of him, because the whole crowd was astonished at his teaching.

At the time of Passover, on the first day of unleavened bread, when the Passover lamb would be sacrificed, the disciples said to Jesus, "Where should we go and get things prepared for you to celebrate Passover?"

And he sent off two of his disciples and said to them, "Go into the city, and a man carrying a water pot will meet you. Follow him. Whichever place he enters, say to the head of that house, 'The teacher says, "Where is my guest room in which I can celebrate Passover with my disciples?"' And he'll show you a spacious upstairs room that is furnished and ready. Prepare that room for us."

And the disciples left and went into the city, and they found everything just as he had told them. And they prepared for Passover.

In the evening Jesus came with his disciples, and they celebrated Passover together. Mary Magdalene was there, and Simon Peter, Andrew, James, and John, with Salome, Arsinoe, Philip, Levi, Judas Thomas, Judas Iscariot, and others. When they arrived, Judas Iscariot greeted Jesus with a kiss, and said to him, "Rabbi!"[37] The other disciples did the same. And as they were eating, Jesus took a loaf of bread, and gave a blessing and broke it into pieces, and offered it to them. And he took a cup of wine, and gave thanks, and offered it to them, and they all drank from it. And he said to them, "I'm telling you the truth, I'll never again drink of the fruit of the vine until the day I drink it anew in the kingdom of God."

And after they sang a hymn, they went out to the Mount of Olives, to a place called Gethsemane. He said to his disciples, "Sit here while I pray."

And he took with him a few of the disciples, and he began to be troubled and filled with anguish. He said to them, "My soul is so sad that I could die. Stay here and stay awake."

And he went on a little farther, and he fell down on the ground and prayed that if possible this trying hour might pass. He said, "Abba, Father, all things are possible for you. Take this cup away from me. But may your will, not my will, be done."

At once, while he was still speaking, a crowd of Roman soldiers and people with swords and clubs appeared, and they laid hands on Jesus and seized him. And Jesus said to them, "Have you come to arrest me, as you would a rebel, with swords and clubs? Day after day I was in the Temple with you, teaching, and you didn't seize me. But what must be must be."

Many of those with Jesus deserted him and ran away. Jesus, however, did not run, but he handed himself over to those who would arrest him.[38]

And they bound Jesus and led him away to the Roman governor Pontius Pilate. And Pilate asked him, "Are you King of the Jews?"

Jesus answered him, "So you say."

A list of charges was brought against Jesus.

Pilate asked him again, "Don't you have an answer to give? Look at all the charges that are brought against you."

Still Jesus gave no answer, and Pilate was astounded. He had Jesus scourged, and turned him over to be crucified.

The soldiers led him away, and they dressed him in a purple robe and put a crown woven of thorns on his head. And they began to salute him: "Hail, King of the Jews." And they struck him on the head with a stick and spat on him, and they bowed down to him. And after they mocked him, they stripped off the purple robe and dressed him in his own clothes. And they led him out to crucify him.

The soldiers brought Jesus to a place called Golgotha, which means the place of the skull. They offered him wine mixed with myrrh, but he refused it. And they crucified him, and divided up his clothes among them, casting lots to see who would get which garment. It was nine o'clock in the morning when they crucified him. The charge against him read "The King of the Jews." And with him they crucified other rebels.

When noon came, darkness came over the whole land until three o'clock. And at three o'clock Jesus shouted out with a loud voice, "Eloi, Eloi, lama sabachthani?" which means, "My God, my God, why have you abandoned me?"

Standing by Jesus' cross were his mother, his mother's sister, Mary the wife of Clopas, and Mary Magdalene, a beloved disciple. Jesus saw his mother and the disciple he loved standing there, and he said to his mother, "Woman, look, your son."

Then he said to the disciple Mary, "Look, your mother." From that moment the disciple took her into her home.[39]

At last Jesus shouted out a loud cry and took his last breath. And the curtain of the Temple was torn in two from top to bottom.

And when the Roman centurion stationed there saw that he had died in this way, he said, "This man was truly a child of God."

The body of Jesus was taken down from the cross, wrapped in a linen shroud, and placed in a rock tomb. When the Sabbath was over, Mary Magdalene and Mary mother of James and Salome went to the tomb, bringing spices so that they might anoint the body of Jesus. He was buried in a tomb with a stone that could be rolled up against the door of the tomb.[40]

The Aftermath

Jesus was gone.

The disciples were upset and wept profoundly, and they said, "How can we go to the gentile world and preach the message of good news about the kingdom of the child of humanity? If they didn't spare him, how will they spare us?"

Mary Magdalene stood up and gave greetings to them all. She said to her brothers and sisters, "Do not weep or be upset or in doubt, for his grace will abide with you all and protect you. Rather, we should praise his greatness, for he has prepared us and made us human."

When Mary said this, she moved their hearts toward the good, and they began to discuss the savior's words.[41]

Peter, however, said to them, "Mary should leave us, for females are not worthy of life."[42]

He expressed his doubts: "Did Jesus really speak with this woman Mary in private without our knowledge? Should we all turn and listen to her? Did he favor her over us?"

Then Mary wept and said to Peter, "My brother Peter, what are you thinking? Do you think I made all this up myself, and that I am telling lies about the savior?"

Levi replied to Peter, "Peter, you are always a hothead. Now I see you arguing against this woman like the adversaries. If the savior made her worthy, who are you to turn her away? Certainly the savior knows her very well. That's why he loved her more than us.

"So, we should be ashamed, and put on perfect humanity and acquire it, as he commanded us, and preach the good news, and not make any rule or law other than what the savior stated."

After he said this, they got up and went out to teach and preach.[43]

Endnotes

1. Cf. Gospel of Thomas Prologue, 1–2.
2. Cf. Gospel of Thomas 46.
3. Cf. Gospel of Thomas 3.
4. Cf. the laughter of Jesus throughout the Gospel of Judas and in other gnostic texts.
5. This entire section is based on Mark 1:1–45.
6. Cf. John 12:6.
7. Cf. Mark 3:13–19.
8. Cf. Gospel of Thomas 61.
9. Cf. Book of Thomas 138.
10. Cf. Gospel of Thomas 99; Mark 3:31–35; Matthew 12:46–50; Luke 8:19–21; Gospel of the Ebionites 5.
11. Cf. Gospel of Thomas 13.
12. Cf. Gospel of Judas 35.
13. Cf. Gospel of Thomas 108.
14. Cf. Gospel of Judas 47.
15. Cf. Gospel of Thomas 15.
16. This section is based on selections from the Sermon on the Mount in Matthew 5:1—7:29 (Q).
17. Cf. Mark 4:2.
18. Cf. Gospel of Thomas 8.
19. Cf. Gospel of Thomas 9; Mark 4:2–9; Matthew 13:3–9; Luke 8:4–8.
20. Cf. Gospel of Thomas 20; Mark 4:30–32; Matthew 13:31–32; Luke 13:18–19.
21. Cf. Gospel of Thomas 21.
22. Cf. Dialogue of the Savior 139.
23. Cf. Pistis Sophia 19.
24. Cf. Gospel of Thomas 57; Matthew 13:24–30.
25. Cf. Gospel of Thomas 63; Luke 12:16–21.
26. Cf. Gospel of Thomas 64; Matthew 22:1–14; Luke 14:16–24.
27. Cf. Gospel of Thomas 65; Mark 12:1–9; Matthew 21:33–41; Luke 20:9–16.
28. Cf. Gospel of Thomas 76; Matthew 13:45–46.
29. Cf. Gospel of Thomas 96; Matthew 13:33; Luke 13:20–21.

30. Cf. Gospel of Thomas 97.

31. Cf. Gospel of Thomas 98.

32. Cf. Gospel of Thomas 107; Matthew 18:12–13; Luke 15:4–7.

33. Cf. Gospel of Thomas 109; Matthew 13:44.

34. Cf. Gospel of Judas 41–42. The first line of this section of text, on rivers, is fragmentary in the manuscript; the reading given here is purely speculative, but hopefully it reflects the spirit of the rest of the lines.

35. This injunction to pay close attention is found throughout early Christian literature.

36. Cf. Gospel of Mary 8–9.

37. Cf. Mark 14:45.

38. Cf. Galatians 2:20. On these scenes of the last days of Jesus, perhaps compare the account of the last days of Socrates in Plato's dialogues, including the *Apology*, the *Crito*, and especially the *Phaedo*.

39. Cf. John 19:25–27.

40. This entire section is based on selections taken from Mark 10–16.

41. Cf. Gospel of Mary 9.

42. Cf. Gospel of Thomas 114.

43. Cf. Gospel of Mary 17–19.

BIBLIOGRAPHY

Aland, Kurt, editor. *Synopsis Quattuor Evangeliorum: Locis parallelis evangeliorum apocryphorum et patrum adhibitis.* 15th rev. ed., 3rd corrected printing. Stuttgart: Deutsche Bibelgesellschaft, 2001, revised 2009. With an Appendix by the Berliner Arbeitskreis für koptisch-gnostische Schriften, "Das Thomas-Evangelium/The Gospel according to Thomas."

Asgeirsson, Jon Ma., Kristin De Troyer, and Marvin W. Meyer, editors. *From Quest to Q: Festschrift James M. Robinson.* Bibliotheca Ephemeridum Theologicarum Lovaniensium 146. Louvain: Peeters, 2000.

Attridge, Harold W. "Greek Equivalents of Two Coptic Phrases: CG I.*1*. 65,9–10 and CG II,2.43.26." *Bulletin of the American Society of Papyrologists* 18 (1981) 27–32.

———. "The Original Text of Gos. Thom., Saying 30." *Bulletin of the American Society of Papyrologists* 16 (1979) 153–57.

Baarda, Tjitze. "Jesus Said: Be Passers-By: On the Meaning and Origin of Logion 42 of the Gospel of Thomas." In *Early Transmission of Words of Jesus: Thomas, Tatian and the Text of the New Testament,* edited by J. Helderman and S. J. Noorda, 179–205. Amsterdam: VU Boekhandel/Uitgeverij, 1983.

Baigent, Michael, Richard Leigh, and Henry Lincoln. *Holy Blood, Holy Grail.* New York: Dell, 1983.

Baker, Aelred. "'Fasting to the World.'" *Journal of Biblical Literature* 84 (1965) 291–94.

———. "Pseudo-Macarius and the Gospel of Thomas." *Vigiliae Christianae* 18 (1964) 215–25.

Barnstone, Willis. *The Restored New Testament: A New Translation with Commentary, Including the Gnostic Gospels Thomas, Mary, and Judas.* New York: Norton, 2009.

Barnstone, Willis, and Marvin Meyer, editors. *Essential Gnostic Scriptures.* Boston: Shambhala, 2010.

———, editors. *The Gnostic Bible.* 2nd ed. Boston: Shambhala, 2009.

Bauer, Johannes B. "Das Jesuswort 'Wer mir nahe ist.'" *Theologische Zeitschrift* 15 (1959) 446–50.

Bauer, Walter. *Orthodoxy and Heresy in Earliest Christianity.* Translated by a team from the Philadelphia Seminar on Christian Origins. Edited by Robert A. Kraft and Gerhard Krodel. Philadelphia: Fortress, 1971.

Bibliography

Bernabé Ubieta, Carmen. *Maria Magdalena: Tradiciones en el Cristianismo Primitivo*. Institución San Jerónimo 27. Estella: Verbo Divino, 1994.

Bethge, Hans-Gebhard, Stephen Emmel, Karen L. King, and Imke Schletterer, editors. *For the Children, Perfect Instruction: Studies in Honor of Hans-Martin Schenke on the Occasion of the Berliner Arbeitskreis für koptisch-gnostische Schriften's Thirtieth Year*. Nag Hammadi and Manichaean Studies 54. Leiden: Brill, 2002.

Blatz, Beate. "The Coptic Gospel of Thomas." In *New Testament Apocrypha*, edited by Wilhelm Schneemelcher, 1.110–33.

Bonner, Campbell. *Studies in Magical Amulets, Chiefly Graeco-Egyptian*. Ann Arbor: University of Michigan Press; London: Oxford University Press, 1950.

Borges, Jorge Luis. "Three Versions of Judas." In *Labyrinths: Selected Stories & Other Writings*, 95–100. New York: New Directions, 1964.

Brakke, David. *The Gnostics: Myth, Ritual, and Diversity in Early Christianity*. Cambridge: Harvard University Press, 2011.

Brankaer, Johanna, and Hans-Gebhard Bethge. *Codex Tchacos: Texte und Analysen*. Texte und Untersuchungen zur Geschichte der altchristlichen Literatur 161. Berlin: de Gruyter, 2007.

Brock, Ann Graham. *Mary Magdalene, the First Apostle: The Struggle for Authority*. Harvard Theological Studies 51. Cambridge: Harvard University Press, 2002.

Brooten, Bernadette. *Women Leaders in the Ancient Synagogue: Inscriptional Evidence and Background Issues*. Brown Judaic Studies 36. Chico, CA: Scholars, 1982.

Brown, Dan. *The Da Vinci Code: A Novel*. New York: Doubleday, 2003.

Brown, Raymond E. "The Gospel of Thomas and St John's Gospel." *New Testament Studies* 9 (1962–63) 155–77.

Buckley, Jorunn Jacobsen. *Female Fault and Fulfillment in Gnosticism*. Studies in Religion. Chapel Hill: University of North Carolina Press, 1986.

Cameron, Ron. "Thomas, Gospel of." In *Anchor Bible Dictionary*, edited by David Noel Freedman, 6:535–40. New York: Doubleday, 1992.

Cameron, Ron, and Arthur J. Dewey, editors. *The Cologne Mani Codex*. Early Christian Literature Series 3. Missoula, MT: Scholars, 1979.

Crum, W. E. *A Coptic Dictionary*. 1939. Reprinted, with a new Foreword by James M. Robinson. Ancient Language Resources. Eugene, OR: Wipf & Stock, 2005.

Cullmann, Oscar. "Das Thomasevangelium und die Frage nach dem Alter der in ihm enthaltenen Tradition." In *Vorträge und Aufsätze*. Zürich: Zwingli, 1960.

Davies, Stevan L. *The Gospel of Thomas and Christian Wisdom*. New York: Seabury, 1983.

DeConick, April D., editor. *The Codex Judas Papers: Proceedings of the International Congress on the Tchacos Codex Held at Rice University, Houston,*

Texas, March 13–16, 2008. Nag Hammadi and Manichaean Studies 71. Leiden: Brill, 2009.

———. *The Original Gospel of Thomas in Translation, with Commentary and New English Translation of the Complete Gospel.* Journal for the Study of the New Testament Supplement Series. London: T. & T. Clark International, 2006.

———. *Recovering the Original Gospel of Thomas: A History of the Gospel and Its Growth.* Early Christianity in Context. London: T. & T. Clark International, 2005.

———. *The Thirteenth Apostle: What the Gospel of Judas Really Says.* New York: Continuum, 2007.

DeConick, April D., and Jarl Fossum. "Stripped before God: A New Interpretation of Logion 37 in the *Gospel of Thomas.*" *Vigiliae Christianae* 45 (1991) 123–50.

de Boer, Esther A. "A Gnostic Mary in the Gospel of Mary?" In *Proceedings of the Seventh International Congress of Coptic Studies,* edited by Jacques van der Vliet, 695–708. Orientalia Lovaniensia Analecta. Louvain: Peeters, 2004.

———. *The Gospel of Mary: Beyond a Gnostic and a Biblical Mary Magdalene.* London: T. & T. Clark International, 2004.

———. "Mary Magdalene and the Disciple Jesus Loved." *Lectio Difficilior* 1 (2000) electronic journal. Online: http://www.lectio.unibe.ch.

———. *Mary Magdalene: Beyond the Myth.* Translated by John Bowden. Harrisburg, PA: Trinity, 1997.

Dehandschutter, B. "La parabole des vignerons homicides (Mc. XII, 1–12) et l'Évangile selon Thomas." In *L'Évangile selon Marc: Tradition et rédaction,* edited by M. Sabbe, 203–19. Bibliotheca ephemeridum theologicarum lovaniensium 34. Gembloux: Duculot, 1974.

Doresse, Jean. *The Secret Books of the Egyptian Gnostics: An Introduction to the Gnostic Coptic Manuscripts Discovered at Chenoboskion.* Translated by Philip Mairet. London: Hollis & Carter, 1960.

Drijvers, Han J. W. "The Acts of Thomas." In *New Testament Apocrypha,* edited by Wilhelm Schneemelcher, 2.322–39.

Ehrman, Bart. *Lost Christianities: The Battle for Scripture and the Faiths We Never Knew.* Oxford: Oxford University Press, 2003.

———. *The Lost Gospel of Judas Iscariot: A New Look at Betrayer and Betrayed.* Oxford: Oxford University Press, 2006.

———. *Lost Scriptures: Books That Did Not Make It into the New Testament.* Oxford: Oxford University Press, 2005.

Eisen, Ute E. *Amtsträgerinnen im frühen Christentum: Epigraphische und literarische Studien.* Forschungen zur Kirchen- und Dogmengeschichte 61. Göttingen: Vandenhoeck & Ruprecht, 1996.

Evans, Craig A., Robert L. Webb, and Richard A. Wiebe, editors. *Nag Hammadi and the Bible: A Synopsis and Index.* New Testament Tools and Studies 18. Leiden: Brill, 1993.

Bibliography

Evelyn-White, Hugh G. *The Sayings of Jesus from Oxyrhynchus*. Cambridge: Cambridge University Press, 1920.

The Facsimile Edition of the Nag Hammadi Codices. Published under the auspices of the Department of Antiquities of the Arab Republic of Egypt in conjunction with the United Nations Educational, Scientific and Cultural Organization. 12 vols. Leiden: Brill, 1972–84.

Fallon, Francis T., and Ron Cameron. "The Gospel of Thomas: A Forschungsbericht and Analysis." In *Aufstieg und Niedergang der römischen Welt*, edited by Hildegard Temporini and Wolfgang Haase, II.25.6: 4195–251. Berlin: de Gruyter, 1988.

Festugière, André-Jean, ed. *Les Actes apocryphes de Jean et de Thomas*. Cahiers d'orientalisme 6. Geneva: Cramer, 1983.

Fitzmyer, Joseph A. "The Oxyrhynchus Logoi of Jesus and the Coptic Gospel according to Thomas." In *Essays on the Semitic Background of the New Testament*, 355–433. London: Chapman, 1971.

Franzmann, Majella. *Jesus in the Nag Hammadi Writings*. Edinburgh: T. & T. Clark, 1996.

Fredriksson, Marianne. *According to Mary Magdalene*. Translated by Joanne Tate. Charlottesville, NC: Hampton Roads, 1999.

Gärtner, Bertil. *The Theology of the Gospel according to Thomas*. Translated by Eric J. Sharpe. New York: Harper & Brothers, 1961.

Gagné, André. "A Critical Note on the Meaning of *apophasis* in *Gospel of Judas* 33:1." *Laval théologique et philosophique* 63 (2007) 377–83.

Gathercole, Simon. *The Gospel of Judas: Rewriting Early Christianity*. Oxford: Oxford University Press, 2007.

Giversen, Søren. "The Palaeography of Oxyrhynchus Papyri 1 and 654–655." Paper presented at the Society of Biblical Literature Annual Meeting, Boston, November 1999.

Grant, Robert M., and David Noel Freedman. *The Secret Sayings of Jesus, with an English Translation of the Gospel of Thomas by William R. Schoedel*. Garden City, NY: Doubleday, 1960.

Grenfell, Bernard P., and Arthur S. Hunt. *LOGIA IESOU: Sayings of Our Lord from an Early Greek Papyrus*. Egyptian Exploration Fund. London: Frowde, 1897.

Grenfell, Bernard P., and Arthur S. Hunt. *New Sayings of Jesus and Fragment of a Lost Gospel from Oxyrhynchus*. Egypt Exploration Fund. London: Frowde, 1904.

Gryson, Roger. *Le ministère des femmes dans l'Église ancienne*. Recherches et synthèses, Section d'histoire. Gembloux: Duculot, 1972.

Gubar, Susan. *Judas: A Biography*. New York and London: Norton, 2009.

Guillaumont, Antoine. "Les sémitismes dans l'Évangile selon Thomas: Essai de classement." In *Studies in Gnosticism and Hellenistic Religions Presented to Gilles Quispel on the Occasion of His 65th Birthday*, edited by R. van der Broek and M. J. Vermaseren, 190–204. Études préliminaires aux religions orientales dans l'empire romain 91. Leiden: Brill, 1981.

———. "Sémitismes dans les logia de Jésus retrouvés à Nag-Hamâdi." *Journal asiatique* 246 (1958) 113–23.

Guillaumont, Antoine, Henri-Charles Puech, Gilles Quispel, Walter Till, and Yassah 'Abd al-Masih, translators. *The Gospel according to Thomas.* Leiden: Brill, 1959.

Haenchen, Ernst. "Die Anthropologie des Thomas-Evangeliums." In *Neues Testament und christliche Existenz: Festschrift für Herbert Braun zum 70. Geburtstag am 4. May 1973,* edited by Hans Dieter Betz and Luise Schott-roff, 207–27. Tübingen: Mohr/Siebeck, 1973.

———. *Die Botschaft des Thomas-Evangeliums.* Theologische Bibliothek Töpel-mann 6. Berlin: Töpelmann, 1961.

Halas, Roman B. *Judas Iscariot: A Scriptural and Theological Study of His Person, His Deeds and His Eternal Lot.* Studies in Sacred Theology 96. Washington, DC: Catholic University Press, 1946.

Harvey, W. W. *Irenaeus, Libros quinque adversus haereses.* 1857. Ridgewood, NJ: Gregg, 1965.

Haskins, Susan. *Mary Magdalen: The Essential History.* London: Random House, 2005.

———. *Mary Magdalen: Myth and Metaphor.* New York: Harcourt Brace, 1993.

Hearon, Holly E. *The Mary Magdalene Tradition: Witness and Counter-Witness.* Collegeville, MN: Liturgical, 2004.

Hedrick, Charles W. "An Anecdotal Argument for the Independence of the *Gospel of Thomas* from the Synoptic Gospels." In *For the Children, Perfect Instruction,* edited by Hans-Gebhard Bethge, Stephen Emmel, Karen L. King, and Imke Schletterer, 113–26.

———. "Thomas and the Synoptics: Aiming at a Consensus." *Second Century* 7 (1989–90) 39–56.

———. *Unlocking the Secrets of the Gospel according to Thomas: A Radical Faith for a New Age.* Eugene, OR: Cascade Books, 2010.

Hedrick, Charles W., and Robert Hodgson Jr., editors. *Nag Hammadi, Gnosti-cism, and Early Christianity.* 1986. Reprinted, Eugene, OR: Wipf & Stock, 2005.

Hofius, Otfried. "Das koptische Thomasevangelium und die Oxyrhynchus-Pa-pyri Nr. 1, 654 und 655." *Evangelische Theologie* 20 (1960) 21–42, 182–92.

Holmén, Tom, editor. *Jesus in Continuum.* Wissenschaftliche Untersuchungen zum Neuen Testament 289. Tübingen: Mohr/Siebeck, 2012.

Ilan, Tal. *Jewish Women in Greco-Roman Palestine: An Inquiry into Image and Status.* Texte und Studien zum Antiken Judentum 44. Tübingen: Mohr/Siebeck, 1995.

Iricinschi, Eduard, Lance Jenott, and Philippa Townsend. "Gospel of Judas." In *The Complete Gospels,* edited by Robert J. Miller, 343–57.

Jackson, Howard M. *The Lion Becomes Man: The Gnostic Leontomorphic Cre-ator and the Platonic Tradition.* Society of Biblical Literature Dissertation Series 81. Atlanta: Scholars, 1985.

Bibliography

Jansen, Katherine L. *The Making of the Magdalene: Preaching and Popular Devotion in the Later Middle Ages.* Princeton: Princeton University Press, 2000.

Jansen, Katherine L. "Maria Magdalena: Apostolorum Apostola." In *Women Preachers and Prophets through Two Millennia of Christianity*, edited by Beverly M. Kienzle and Pamela J. Walker, 57–96. Berkeley: University of California Press, 1998.

Jantzen, Grace M. *Power, Gender, and Christian Mysticism.* Cambridge Studies in Ideology and Religion 8. Cambridge: Cambridge University Press, 1997.

Jensen, Anne. *Gottes selbstbewusste Töchter: Frauenemanzipation im frühen Christentum?* Freiburg: Herder, 1992.

Jenott, Lance. *The Gospel of Judas: Text, Translation, and Historical Interpretation of the Betrayer's Gospel.* Studies and Texts in Antiquity and Christianity. Tübingen: Mohr/Siebeck, 2011.

Jonas, Hans. *The Gnostic Religion: The Message of the Alien God and the Beginnings of Christianity.* 2nd ed. Boston: Beacon, 1963.

———. *Gnosis und spätantiker Geist: Die mythologische Gnosis.* 3rd ed. Forschungen zur Religion und Literatur des Alten und Neuen Testaments 51. Göttingen: Vandenhoeck & Ruprecht, 1964.

Jones, F. Stanley, editor. *Which Mary? The Marys of Early Christian Tradition.* SBL Symposium Series 19. Atlanta: Society of Biblical Literature, 2002.

Jusino, Ramon K. "Mary Magdalene: Author of the Fourth Gospel?" Website, posted in 1998. Online: http://www.Beloved Disciple.org.

Kasser, Rodolphe. *L'Évangile selon Thomas: Présentation et commentaire théologique.* Bibliothèque théologique. Neuchâtel: Delachaux et Niestlé, 1961.

Kasser, Rodolphe, Marvin Meyer, Gregor Wurst, and François Gaudard, editors. *The Gospel of Judas.* Washington, DC: National Geographic Society, 2006 (1st ed.), 2008 (2nd ed.).

Kasser, Rodolphe, Marvin Meyer, Gregor Wurst, and François Gaudard, editors. *The Gospel of Judas, Together with the Letter of Peter to Philip, James, and a Book of Allogenes, from Codex Tchacos: Critical Edition.* Washington, DC: National Geographic Society, 2007.

Kazantzakis, Nikos. *The Last Temptation of Christ.* Translated by P. A. Bien. New York: Simon & Schuster, 1960.

Kee, Howard C. "'Becoming a Child' in the Gospel of Thomas." *Journal of Biblical Literature* 82 (1963) 307–14.

Kemner, Heinrich. *Judas Iskariot: Zwischen Nachfolge und Verrat.* Stuttgart: Neuhausen, 1988.

Khalidi, Tarif, editor. *The Muslim Jesus: Sayings and Stories in Islamic Literature.* Cambridge: Harvard University Press, 2001.

King, Karen L. "The Gospel of Mary." In *The Complete Gospels*, edited by Robert J. Miller, 333–42.

———. "The Gospel of Mary Magdalene." In *Searching the Scriptures: A Feminist Commentary*, edited by Elisabeth Schüssler Fiorenza, 601–34.

———. *The Gospel of Mary of Magdala: Jesus and the First Woman Apostle.* Santa Rosa, CA: Polebridge, 2003.

———, editor. *Images of the Feminine in Gnosticism.* Studies in Antiquity and Christianity. Philadelphia: Fortress, 1988.

———. *What Is Gnosticism?* Cambridge: Belknap, 2003.

———. "Why All the Controversy? Mary in the *Gospel of Mary.*" In *Which Mary?*, edited by F. Stanley Jones, 53–74.

Klassen, William. *Judas: Betrayer or Friend of Jesus?* Minneapolis: Fortress, 1996.

———. "Judas Iscariot." In *The Anchor Bible Dictionary*, edited by David Noel Freedman, 3:1091–96. New York: Doubleday, 1992.

Klauck, Hans-Josef. *Judas—Ein Jünger des Herrn.* Quaestiones Disputatae 111. Freiburg: Herder, 1987.

Klijn, A. F. J. *The Acts of Thomas: Introduction—Text—Commentary.* Supplements to Novum Testamentum 5. Leiden: Brill, 1962.

———. "Christianity in Edessa and the Gospel of Thomas." *Novum Testamentum* 14 (1972) 70–77.

———. *Edessa, die Stadt des Apostels Thomas: Das älteste Christentum in Syrien.* Neukirchener Studienbücher 4. Neukirchen-Vluyn: Erziehungsverein, 1965.

———. *Seth in Jewish, Christian, and Gnostic Literature.* Supplements to Novum Testamentum 46. Leiden: Brill, 1977.

———. "The 'Single One' in the Gospel of Thomas." *Journal of Biblical Literature* 81 (1962) 271–78.

Kloppenborg, John S., Marvin W. Meyer, Stephen J. Patterson, and Michael G. Steinhauser. *Q-Thomas Reader.* Sonoma, CA: Polebridge, 1990.

Koester, Helmut. *Ancient Christian Gospels: Their History and Development.* Philadelphia: Trinity, 1990.

Krosney, Herb. *The Lost Gospel: The Quest for the Gospel of Judas Iscariot.* Washington, DC: National Geographic Society, 2006.

Krosney, Herb, Marvin Meyer, and Gregor Wurst. "Preliminary Report on New Fragments of Codex Tchacos." *Early Christianity* 1 (2010) 282–94.

Kuntzmann, Raymond. *Le Livre de Thomas (NH II,7): Texte établi et présenté.* Bibliothèque copte de Nag Hammadi, Section "Textes" 16. Louvain: Peeters, 1986.

Layton, Bentley. *The Gnostic Scriptures: A New Translation with Annotations and Introductions.* Garden City, NY: Doubleday, 1987.

———, editor. *Nag Hammadi Codex II,2–7, Together with XIII,2*, Brit. Lib. Or. 4926(1), and P. Oxy. 1, 654, 655.* 2 vols. Nag Hammadi Studies 20–21. Leiden: Brill, 1989.

———, editor. *The Rediscovery of Gnosticism: Proceedings of the International Conference on Gnosticism at Yale, New Haven, Connecticut, March 28–31, 1978.* Studies in the History of Religions—Supplements to Numen 41. Leiden: Brill, 1980–81.

Bibliography

Letsch-Brunner, Silvia. *Marcella, Discipula et Magistra: Auf den Spuren einer römischen Christin des 4. Jahrhunderts.* Beihefte zur Zeitschrift für die neutestamentliche Wissenschaft und die Kunde der älteren Kirche 91. Berlin: de Gruyter, 1998.

Lührmann, Dieter. "Die griechischen Fragmente des Mariaevangeliums POxy 3525 und PRyl 463." *Novum Testamentum* 30 (1988) 321–38.

Maccoby, Hyam. *Judas Iscariot and the Myth of Jewish Evil.* New York: Free Press, 1992.

MacDonald, Dennis R. *The Homeric Epics and the Gospel of Mark.* New Haven: Yale University Press, 2000.

Mahé, Jean-Pierre, and Paul-Hubert Poirier, editors. Écrits gnostiques. Bibliothèque de la Pléiade. Paris: Gallimard, 2007.

Maisch, Ingrid. *Maria Magdalena zwischen Verachtung und Verehrung: Das Bild einer Frau im Spiegel der Jahrhunderte.* Freiburg: Herder, 1996.

Marcovich, M. "Textual Criticism on the Gospel of Thomas." *Journal of Theological Studies* n.s. 20 (1969) 53–74.

Marjanen, Antti. *The Woman Jesus Loved: Mary Magdalene in the Nag Hammadi Library and Related Documents.* Nag Hammadi and Manichaean Studies 40. Leiden: Brill, 1996.

———, editor. *Was There a Gnostic Religion?* Publications of the Finnish Exegetical Society 87. Göttingen: Vandenhoeck & Ruprecht, 2005.

Marjanen, Antti, and Petri Luomanen, editors. *A Companion to Second-Century Christian "Heretics."* Supplements to Vigiliae Christianae 76. Leiden: Brill, 2005.

McGuire, Anne. "Women, Gender, and Gnosis in Gnostic texts and Traditions." In *Women and Christian Origins,* edited by Ross Shepard Kraemer and Mary Rose D'Angelo, 257–99. Oxford: Oxford University Press, 1999.

Ménard, Jacques-É. *L'Évangile selon Thomas.* Nag Hammadi Studies 5. Leiden: Brill, 1975.

Meyer, Marvin. *The Gnostic Discoveries: The Impact of the Nag Hammadi Library.* San Francisco: HarperOne, 2005.

———. *The Gnostic Gospels of Jesus.* San Francisco: HarperOne, 2005.

———. *The Gospel of Judas: On a Night with Judas Iscariot.* Eugene, OR: Cascade Books, 2011.

———. *The Gospel of Thomas: The Hidden Sayings of Jesus.* San Francisco: HarperSanFrancisco, 1992.

———. "*Gospel of Thomas* Logion 114 Revisited." In *For the Children, Perfect Instruction,* edited by Hans-Gebhard Bethge, Stephen Emmel, Karen L. King, and Imke Schletterer, 101–11. Reprinted in Marvin Meyer, *Secret Gospels,* 96–106.

———. *The Gospels of Mary: The Secret Tradition of Mary Magdalene, the Companion of Jesus.* San Francisco: HarperSanFrancisco, 2004.

———. "Jesus, Judas Iscariot, and the *Gospel of Judas.*" In *Jesus in Continuum,* edited by Tom Holmén, 115–32.

————. *Judas: The Definitive Collection of Gospels and Legends about the Infamous Apostle of Jesus*. San Francisco: HarperOne, 2007.

————. "Making Mary Male: The Categories 'Male' and 'Female' in the *Gospel of Thomas*." *New Testament Studies* 31 (1985) 544–70. Reprinted in Marvin Meyer, *Secret Gospels*, 76–95.

————, editor. *The Nag Hammadi Scriptures: The International Edition*. San Francisco: HarperOne, 2007.

————. *Secret Gospels: Essays on Thomas and the Secret Gospel of Mark*. London: Trinity Press International, 2003.

————. *The Unknown Sayings of Jesus*. Boston: Shambhala, 1998.

————. "When the Sethians Were Young: The Gospel of Judas in the Second Century." In *The Codex Judas Papers*, edited by April D. DeConick, 57–73.

————. "Whom Did Jesus Love Most? Beloved Disciples in John and Other Gospels." In *The Legacy of John: Second Century Reception of the Fourth Gospel*, edited by Tuomas Rasimus, 73–91. Novum Testamentum Supplements 132. Leiden: Brill, 2009.

Meyer, Marvin, and Charles Hughes, editors. *Jesus Then and Now: Images of Jesus in History and Christology*. London: Trinity, 2001.

Meyers, Carol, Toni Craven, and Ross Shepard Kraemer, editors. *Women in Scripture: A Dictionary of Named and Unnamed Women in the Hebrew Bible, the Apocryphal/Deuterocanonical Books, and the New Testament*. Grand Rapids: Eerdmans, 2001.

Miller, Robert J., editor. *The Complete Gospels*. 4th ed. Salem, OR: Polebridge, 2010.

Mirecki, Paul A. "Coptic Manichaean Psalm 278 and Gospel of Thomas 37." In *Manichaica Selecta: Studies Presented to Professor Julien Ries on the Occasion of His Seventieth Birthday*, edited by Alois van Tongerloo and Søren Giversen, 243–62. Manichaean Studies 1. Louvain: International Association of Manichaean Studies/Center of the History of Religions, 1991.

Mohri, Erika. *Maria Magdalena: Frauenbilder in Evangelientexten des 1. bis 3. Jahrhunderts*. Marburger theologische Studien 63. Marburg: Elwert, 2000.

Most, Glenn W. *Doubting Thomas*. Cambridge: Harvard University Press, 2005.

Nagel, Peter. "Das Evangelium des Judas." *Zeitschrift für die neutestamentliche Wissenschaft* 98 (2007) 213–76.

————. "Das Evangelium des Judas—zwei Jahre später." *Zeitschrift für die neutestamentliche Wissenschaft* 100 (2009) 101–38.

Neller, Kenneth V. "Diversity in the Gospel of Thomas: Clues for a New Direction?" *The Second Century* 7 (1989–90) 1–18.

Oort, Johannes van. *Het evangelie van Judas: Inleiding, vertaling, toelichting*. Kampen: Uitgeverij Ten Have, 2006.

Paffenroth, Kim. *Judas: Images of the Lost Disciple*. Louisville: Westminster John Knox, 2001.

Pagels, Elaine H. *Beyond Belief: The Secret Gospel of Thomas*. New York: Random House, 2003.

————. *The Gnostic Gospels*. New York: Random House, 1979.

Bibliography

Pagels, Elaine H., and Karen L. King. *Reading Judas: The Gospel of Judas and the Shaping of Christianity*. New York: Viking, 2007.

Parrott, Douglas M., editor. *Nag Hammadi Codices V, 2–5 and VI with Papyrus Berolinensis 8502,1 and 4*. Nag Hammadi Studies 11. Leiden: Brill, 1979.

Pasquier, Anne. *L'Évangile selon Marie (BG 1)*. Bibliothèque copte de Nag Hammadi, Section "Textes" 10. Louvain: Peeters, 1983.

Patterson, Stephen J. *The Gospel of Thomas and Jesus*. Sonoma, CA: Polebridge, 1993.

———. "Wisdom in Q and Thomas." In *In Search of Wisdom: Essays in Memory of John G. Gammie*, edited by Leo G. Perdue, Bernard Brandon Scott, and William Johnston Wiseman, 187–221. Louisville: Westminster John Knox, 1993.

Patterson, Stephen J., James M. Robinson, and Hans-Gebhard Bethge. *The Fifth Gospel: The Gospel of Thomas Comes of Age*. Harrisburg, PA: Trinity, 1998 (1st edition); 2011 (2nd edition).

Pearson, Birger A. *Ancient Gnosticism: Traditions and Literature*. Minneapolis: Fortress, 2007.

———. *Gnosticism and Christianity in Roman and Coptic Egypt*. Studies in Antiquity and Christianity. London: T. & T. Clark International, 2004.

———. *Gnosticism, Judaism, and Egyptian Christianity*. Studies in Antiquity and Christianity. Minneapolis: Fortress, 1990.

———. "Judas Iscariot and the Gospel of Judas." Institute for Antiquity and Christianity Occasional Paper 51. Claremont, CA: Institute for Antiquity and Christianity, 2007.

Perrin, Nicholas. *Thomas and Tatian: The Relationship between the Gospel of Thomas and the Diatessaron*. Academia Biblica 5. Atlanta: Society of Biblical Literature, 2002.

Petersen, Silke. *"Zerstört die Werke der Weiblichkeit!" Maria Magdalena, Salome und andere Jüngerinnen Jesu in christlich-gnostische Schriften*. Nag Hammadi and Manichaean Studies 48. Leiden: Brill, 1999.

Piñero, Antonio, and Sofía Torallas. *El Evangelio de Judas*. Puzzle: Enigmas Historico. Madrid: Vector, 2006.

Plisch, Uwe-Karsten. *The Gospel of Thomas: Original Text and Commentary*. Translated by Gesine Schenke Robinson. Stuttgart: Deutsche Bibelgesellschaft, 2008.

Pokorný, Petr. *A Commentary on the Gospel of Thomas: From Interpretations to the Interpreted*. Jewish and Christian Texts in Contexts and Related Studies 5. London: T. & T. Clark International, 2009.

Pomeroy, Sarah B. *Goddesses, Whores, Wives, and Slaves: Women in Classical Antiquity*. New York: Schocken, 1975, 1995.

Puech, Henri-Charles. "Un logion de Jésus sur bandelette funéraire." *Revue de l'histoire des religions* 147 (1955) 126–29.

Quispel, Gilles. *Gnostic Studies II*. Uitgaven van het Nederlands Historisch-Archaeologisch Instituut te Istanbul 34/2. Istanbul: Nederlands Historisch-Archaeologisch Instituut te Istanbul, 1975.

————. *Makarius, das Thomasevangelium und das Lied von der Perle*. Novum Testamentum Supplements 15. Leiden: Brill, 1967.

————. *Tatian and the Gospel of Thomas: Studies in the History of the Western Diatessaron*. Leiden: Brill, 1975.

Riley, Gregory J. *Resurrection Reconsidered: Thomas and John in Controversy*. Minneapolis: Fortress, 1995.

————. *The River of God: A New History of Christian Origins*. San Francisco: HarperSanFrancisco, 2001.

Robinson, James M. "From the Cliff to Cairo: The Story of the Discoverers and Middlemen of the Nag Hammadi Codices." In *Colloque international sur les textes de Nag Hammadi (Québec, 22–25 août 1978)*, edited by Bernard Barc, 21–58. Bibliothèque copte de Nag Hammadi, Section "Études" 1. Louvain: Peeters, 1981.

————. "The Jung Codex: The Rise and Fall of a Monopoly." *Religious Studies Review* 3 (1977) 17–30.

————. "LOGOI SOPHON: On the Gattung of Q." In *Trajectories through Early Christianity*, edited by James M. Robinson and Helmut Koester, 71–113.

————, editor. *The Nag Hammadi Library in English*. 3rd ed. San Francisco: HarperSanFrancisco, 1988.

————. "Nag Hammadi: The First Fifty Years." In Stephen J. Patterson, James M. Robinson, and Hans-Gebhard Bethge, *The Fifth Gospel* (1st ed.), 77–110. Republished in the 2nd ed. as "The Story of the Nag Hammadi Library," 67–96.

————. "On Bridging the Gulf from Q to the Gospel of Thomas (or Vice Versa)." In *Nag Hammadi, Gnosticism, and Early Christianity*, edited by Charles W. Hedrick and Robert Hodgson, Jr., 127–75.

————. *The Secrets of Judas: The Story of the Misunderstood Disciple and His Lost Gospel*. San Francisco: HarperOne, 2006.

Robinson, James M., and Helmut Koester. *Trajectories through Early Christianity*. 1971. Reprinted, Eugene, OR: Wipf & Stock, 2006.

Rudolph, Kurt. *Gnosis: The Nature and History of Gnosticism*. English translation edited by Robert McLachlan Wilson. San Francisco: HarperSanFrancisco, 1987.

————. "Der gnostische 'Dialog' als literarisches Genus." In *Probleme der koptischen Literatur*, edited by Peter Nagel, 85–107. Wissenschaftliche Beiträge K2. Halle-Wittenberg: Martin-Luther-Universität, 1968.

Ruether, Rosemary Radford. "Misogynism and Virginal Feminism in the Fathers of the Church." In *Religion and Sexism: Images of Women in the Jewish and Christian Traditions*, edited by Rosemary Radford Ruether, 150–83. New York: Simon & Schuster, 1974.

————. "Mothers of the Church: Ascetic Women in the Late Patristic Age." In *Women of Spirit: Female Leadership in the Jewish and Christian Traditions*, edited by Rosemary Radford Ruether and E. McLaughlin, 69–98. New York: Simon & Schuster, 1979.

Ruschmann, Susanne. *Maria von Magdala im Johannesevangelium: Jüngerin, Zeugin, Lebensbotin*. Neutestamentliche Abhandlungen N.F. 40. Münster: Aschendorf, 2002.

Schaberg, Jane. "How Mary Magdalene Became a Whore: Mary Magdalene Is in Fact the Primary Witness to the Fundamental Data of Early Christian Faith." *Bible Review* 8/5 (1992) 30–37, 51–52.

———. *The Resurrection of Mary Magdalene: Legends, Apocrypha, and the Christian Testament*. New York: Continuum, 2002.

Schenke, Hans-Martin. "The Book of Thomas (NHC II.7): A Revision of a Pseudepigraphical Epistle of Jacob the Contender." In *The New Testament and Gnosis: Essays in Honour of Robert McL. Wilson*, edited by A. H. B. Logan and A. J. M. Wedderburn, 213–28. Edinburgh: T. & T. Clark, 1983.

———. "The Function and Background of the Beloved Disciple in the Gospel of John." In *Nag Hammadi, Gnosticism, and Early Christianity*, edited by Charles W. Hedrick and Robert Hodgson, Jr., 111–25.

———. "The Phenomenon and Significance of Gnostic Sethianism." In *The Rediscovery of Gnosticism*, edited by Bentley Layton, 2:588–616.

———. "Das sethianische System nach Nag-Hammadi-Handschriften." In *Studia Coptica*, edited by Peter Nagel, 165–73. Berliner Byzantinische Arbeiten 45. Berlin: Akademie, 1974.

———. *Das Thomas-Buch (Nag-Hammadi-Codex II,7): Neu herausgegeben, übersezt und erklärt*. Texte und Untersuchungen 138. Berlin: Akademie, 1989.

Schenke, Hans-Martin, Hans-Gebhard Bethge, and Ursula Ulrike Kaiser, editors. *Nag Hammadi Deutsch*. 2 vols. Die Griechischen Christlichen Schriftsteller der ersten Jahrhunderte, N.F. 8, 12. Berlin: de Gruyter, 2001, 2003.

Schenke Robinson, Gesine. "The Relationship of the *Gospel of Judas* to the New Testament and to Sethianism, Appended by a New English Translation of the *Gospel of Judas*." *Journal of Coptic Studies* 10 (2008) 63–98.

Schneemelcher, Wilhelm, editor. *New Testament Apocrypha*. English translation edited by Robert McLachlan Wilson. 2 vols. Louisville: Westminster John Knox, 1991–92.

Scholem, Gershom. *Jewish Gnosticism, Merkabah Mysticism, and Talmudic Tradition*. New York: Jewish Theological Seminary of America, 1960.

Scholer, David M. *Nag Hammadi Bibliography 1948–1969*. Nag Hammadi Studies 1. Leiden: Brill, 1971.

———. *Nag Hammadi Bibliography 1970–1994*. Nag Hammadi Studies 32. Leiden: Brill, 1997.

Schrage, Wolfhart. *Das Verhältnis des Thomas-Evangeliums zur synoptischen Tradition und zu den koptischen Evangelien-Übersetzungen, Zugleich ein Beitrag zur gnostischen Synoptikerdeutung*. Beihefte zur Zeitschrift für die neutestamentliche Wissenschaft 29. Berlin: Töpelmann, 1964.

Schröter, Jens. *Erinnerung an Jesu Worte: Studien zur Rezeption der Logienüber-lieferung in Markus, Q und Thomas.* Wissenschaftliche Untersuchungen zum Neuen Testament 76. Neukirchen: Neukirchener, 1997.

Schüssler Fiorenza, Elisabeth, editor. *Searching the Scriptures: A Feminist Commentary.* New York: Crossroad, 1993–94.

Schwager, Raymund. *Must There Be Scapegoats? Violence and Redemption in the Bible.* Translated by Maria L. Assad. San Francisco: Harper & Row, 1987.

Schwarz, Günter. *Jesus und Judas: Aramaistische Untersuchungen zur Jesus-Judas Überlieferung der Evangelien und der Apostelgeschichte.* Beiträge zur Wissenschaft vom Alten und Neuen Testament 123. Stuttgart: Kohlhammer, 1988.

Scopello, Madeleine. *Femme, gnose et manichéisme: De l'espace mythique au territoire du réel.* Nag Hammadi and Manichaean Studies 53. Leiden: Brill, 2005.

———, editor. *Gnosis and Revelation: Ten Studies on Codex Tchacos.* Revista di Storia e Letteratura Religiosa 44. Florence: Olschki, 2009.

———, editor. *The Gospel of Judas in Context: Proceedings of the First International Conference on the Gospel of Judas, Paris, Sorbonne, October 27th–28th 2006.* Nag Hammadi and Manichaean Studies 62. Leiden: Brill, 2008.

———. "Jewish and Greek Heroines in the Nag Hammadi Library." In *Images of the Feminine in Gnosticism*, edited by Karen L. King, 71–90.

Segal, Judah Benzion. *Edessa, 'The Blessed City.'* Oxford: Clarendon, 1970.

Seim, Turid K. *The Double Message: Patterns of Gender in Luke-Acts.* Translated by Brian McNeil. Studies of the New Testament and Its World. Edinburgh: T. & T. Clark, 1994.

Sevrin, Jean-Marie. *Le dossier baptismal séthien: Études sur la sacramentaire gnostique.* Bibliothèque copte de Nag Hammadi, Section "Études" 2. Québec: Les Presses de l'Université Laval, 1986.

Sieber, John H. "The *Gospel of Thomas* and the New Testament." In *Gospel Origins and Christian Beginnings: In Honor of James M. Robinson*, edited by James E. Goehring, Charles W. Hedrick, Jack T. Sanders, and Hans Dieter Betz, 64–73. Sonoma, CA: Polebridge, 1990.

Smith, Jonathan Z. "The Garments of Shame." *History of Religions* 5 (1965–66) 217–38. Reprinted in *Map Is Not Territory: Studies in the History of Religions*, 1–23. Studies in Judaism in Late Antiquity 23. Leiden: Brill, 1978.

Snodgrass, Klyne R. "The Gospel of Thomas: A Secondary Gospel." *Second Century* 7 (1989–90) 19–38.

Spong, John Shelby. *Liberating the Gospels: Reading the Bible with Jewish Eyes.* San Francisco: HarperOne, 1996.

Starbird, Margaret. *The Woman with the Alabaster Jar: Mary Magdalen and the Holy Grail.* Santa Fe, NM: Bear & Company, 1993.

Suarez, Philippe de. *L'Évangile selon Thomas: Traducion, Présentation et Commentaires.* Marsanne: Métanoïa, 1975.

Synek, Eva M. "Die andere Maria: Zum Bild der Maria von Magdala in den östlichen Kirchentraditionen." *Oriens Christianus* 79 (1994) 181–96.

Bibliography

Tardieu, Michel. *Écrits gnostiques: Codex de Berlin*. Sources gnostiques et mani-
chéennes 1. Paris: Cerf, 1984.

Till, Walter C., and Hans-Martin Schenke. *Die gnostischen Schriften des koptischen Papyrus Berolinensis 8502*. 2nd ed. Texte und Untersuchungen 60.
Berlin: Akademie, 1972.

Torjesen, Karen Jo. *When Women Were Priests: Women's Leadership in the Early
Church and the Scandal of Their Subordination in the Rise of Christianity*.
San Francisco: HarperSanFrancisco, 1993.

Tuckett, Christopher M. *Nag Hammadi and the Gospel Tradition*. Edinburgh:
T. & T. Clark, 1986.

Tuckett, Christopher M. "Das Thomasevangelium und die synoptischen Evangelien." *Berliner theologische Zeitschrift* 12 (1995) 186–200.

Turner, H. E. W., and Hugh Montefiore. *Thomas and the Evangelists*. Studies in
Biblical Theology 35. Naperville: Allenson, 1962.

Turner, John D. *The Book of Thomas the Contender from Codex II of the Cairo
Gnostic Library from Nag Hammadi (CG II,7): The Coptic Text with Translation, Introduction and Commentary*. Society of Biblical Literature Dissertation Series 23. Missoula, MT: Scholars, 1975.

Turner, John D. "A New Link in the Syrian Judas Thomas Tradition." In *Essays
on Nag Hammadi in Honour of Alexander Böhlig*, edited by Martin Krause,
109–19. Nag Hammadi Studies 3. Leiden: Brill, 1972.

———. "The Sethian Baptismal Rite." In *Coptica, Gnostica, Manichaica: Mé-
langes offerts à Wolf-Peter Funk à l'occasion de son soixantième anniver-
saire*, edited by Paul-Hubert Poirier. Bibliothèque copte de Nag Hammadi,
Section "Études" 8. Louvain: Peeters, 2005.

———. "Sethian Gnosticism: A Literary History." In *Nag Hammadi, Gnosticism, and Early Christianity*, edited by Charles W. Hedrick and Robert
Hodgson, Jr., 55–86.

———. "Sethian Gnosticism and Johannine Christianity." In *Theology and
Christology in the Fourth Gospel: Essays by the Members of the SNTS Jo-
hannine Writings Seminar*, edited by Gilbert van Belle, Jan Gabriël van der
Watt, and P. J. Maritz, 399–433. Bibliotheca Ephemeridum Theologicarum
Lovaniensium 184. Louvain: Louvain University Press/Peeters, 2005.

———. *Sethian Gnosticism and the Platonic Tradition*. Bibliothèque de Nag
Hammadi, Section "Études" 6. Louvain: Peeters, 2001.

Uro, Risto, editor. *Thomas at the Crossroads: Essays on the Gospel of Thomas*.
Edinburgh: T. & T. Clark, 1998.

Valantasis, Richard. *The Gospel of Thomas*. New Testament Readings. London:
Routledge, 1997.

Vielhauer, Philipp. "ANAPAUSIS: Zum gnostischen Hintergrund des Thoma-
sevangeliums." In *Apophoreta: Festschrift für Ernst Haenchen zu seinem
siebzigsten Geburtstag am 10. Dezember 1964*, edited by Walter Eltester
and Franz Heinrich Kettler, 281–99. Beihefte zur Zeitschrift für die neutestamentliche Wissenschaft 30. Berlin: Töpelmann, 1964.

Vliet, Jacques van der. "Judas and the Stars: Philological Notes on the Newly Published Gospel of Judas (GosJud, Codex Gnosticus Maghâgha 3)." *Journal of Juristic Papyrology* 36 (2006) 137–52.

Vogler, Werner. *Judas Iskarioth: Untersuchungen zu Tradition und Redaktion von Texten des Neuen Testaments und außerkanonischer Schriften.* Theologische Arbeiten 42. Berlin: Evangelischer Verlag, 1983, 2nd ed. 1985.

Wagner, Harald, editor. *Judas Iskariot: Menschliches oder Heilsgeschlichtliches Drama?* Frankfurt: Knecht, 1985.

Waldstein, Michael, and Frederik Wisse, editors. *The Apocryphon of John: Synopsis of Nag Hammadi Codices II,1; III,1; and IV,1 with BG 8502,2.* Nag Hammadi and Manichaean Studies 33. Leiden: Brill, 1985.

Williams, Michael A. *The Immovable Race: A Gnostic Designation and the Theme of Stability in Late Antiquity.* Nag Hammadi Studies 29. Leiden: Brill, 1985.

Williams, Michael A. *Rethinking "Gnosticism": An Argument for Dismantling a Dubious Category.* Princeton: Princeton University Press, 1996.

———. "Sethianism." In *A Companion to Second-Century Christian "Heretics,"* edited by Antti Marjanen and Petri Luomanen, 32–63.

———. "Stability as a Soteriological Theme in Gnosticism." In *The Rediscovery of Gnosticism*, edited by Bentley Layton, 2.819–29.

Wilson, R. McL. *Studies in the Gospel of Thomas.* London: Mowbray, 1960.

Wright, N.T. *Judas and the Gospel of Judas: Have We Missed the Truth About Christianity?* Grand Rapids: Baker, 2006.

Wurst, Gregor. "Weitere neue Fragmente aus Codex Tchacos: Zum 'Buch des Allogenes' und zu *Corpus Hermeticum* XIII." Forthcoming.

Zöckler, Thomas. *Jesu Lehren im Thomasevangelium.* Nag Hammadi and Manichaean Studies 47. Leiden: Brill, 1999.

INDEX OF ANCIENT TEXTS

Mark

✆

Gregory the Great, *Homilies*

Hippolytus, *Refutation of All Heresies*

Holy Book of the Great Invisible Spirit

Ignatius of Antioch
To Polycarp

To the Smyrnaeans

〜

Rabbinic Literature